Birds, Boots and Butties
Anglesey

Birds, Boots and Butties
Anglesey

Ruth Miller

Ruth Miller has been a keen birder for much of her life. Together with her partner, Alan Davies, Ruth gave up her home and her job to spend a year travelling the world following her passion for birding. Together they set a new world record for the highest number of bird species seen in a single calendar year: 4,341 species in total in 27 countries around the world! Visit **www.thebiggesttwitch.com** to find out more about their adventures.

First published in 2009

ISBN: 978-1-84524-148-3

Cover design: Carreg Gwalch

Published by Llygad Gwalch,
12 Iard yr Orsaf, Llanrwst, Wales LL26 0EH
tel: 01492 624031
fax: 01492 641502
email: books@carreg-gwalch.com
website: www.carreg-gwalch.com

Contents

Introduction

Birds, Boots and Butties:

Where to walk, watch birds and enjoy a great cuppa on Anglesey!

Imagine you've been out all afternoon enjoying a bracing walk along the stunning Anglesey coast at Cemlyn Bay. You've had the wind in your hair blowing away the cobwebs and have splashed with abandon through puddles in your walking boots. You've enjoyed close-up views of Common Terns flying to and fro bringing a constant stream of fish to their mates on the nest, and you've even spotted some Grey Seals basking on rocks just offshore. Now all you need to complete your perfect day is a nice hot cup of tea or coffee. But you're in the middle of the countryside – so where can you go? *Birds, Boots and Butties Anglesey* has the answer, and will take you straight to the nearest tea room, café or coffee shop!

The inspiration for *Birds, Boots and Butties* came to me while out birding in northern Wales one weekend, and it combines three of my personal passions: birding, walking, and afternoon tea. For me, nothing rounds off a great walk full of exciting wildlife experiences better than a hot cup of tea and a piece of cake!

We are not short of beautiful places to walk on Anglesey. We're spoiled for choice, with breathtaking cliffs and gently shelving beaches, marching conifer forests and intimate deciduous woodland, all within easy reach. As a result of this varied habitat, Anglesey (*Ynys Môn* in Welsh) is blessed too with a wide range of bird species: raptors, seabirds, waders, moorland and woodland birds; all can be enjoyed here across the seasons if you know where to look. But finding where to go for refreshment after a wildlife-rich walk can be even more challenging, as the tearooms and cafés of Wales can sometimes be hard to find.

Was I the only one with this problem? I did some research amongst friends and family and found that I wasn't unique. Other people too enjoyed a country walk watching wildlife, but good refreshment could sometimes be more elusive than the wildlife itself. And so the idea for *Birds, Boots and Butties* was born, and I took it upon myself to thoroughly research all aspects of birding, walking and eating in northern Wales.

All the walks featured in this book have the magic combination of good walking, great birds, and a tearoom or café to suit every taste. The walks are spread across the island of Anglesey from South Stack RSPB Reserve in the north-west to Penmon in the south-east. This is a selection of my personal favourites, and I have aimed to include a variety of length, difficulty, walking terrain and habitat. Each walk covers one of the best sites for birdwatching on Anglesey, ensuring that you not only have an enjoyable walk, but a great birdwatching experience at the same time. And every walk can be completed with a visit to a local tearoom or café either at the beginning, the end, or en route. In a handful of cases the nearest café may be a few minutes' car journey away.

The descriptions of the walks follow the same pattern every time. To help you choose your walk, there is the distance to be walked and an indication of the time needed, as well as specific comments about the terrain. I take you on a step-by-step guide through the walk itself, pointing out items of local interest as we go along, and there's a map for each walk to support the written directions. I have been able to draw upon the experience of local birding experts to make sure that only the best walks for birds are included. As well as giving a guide to what specific birds to look out for through the seasons of the year, I point out where on your walk you are most likely to see them. While I can't provide a cast-iron guarantee that you will see all the birds on your visit, I can help you maximise your chances of success.

Lastly, I include details of where to find the nearest tearoom or café. I have steered clear of making personal comments on the food and drink provided, as my idea of the perfect cuppa may not be yours, but I am sure that you will be able to enjoy a wide range of drinks and snacks at all the venues listed, as they have been tested personally! (All details correct at time of writing.)

So whether you like to walk, watch wildlife, or just eat and drink, *Birds, Boots and Butties Anglesey* has something for you. If you'd like to enjoy the same on the mainland, look out for *Birds, Boots and Butties Conwy Valley/Eastern Snowdonia*. Enjoy!

Ruth Miller

Foreword

Having been lucky enough to travel extensively throughout the UK in search of birds – literally from the Shetland Isles in the north to the Isles of Scilly in the south – I can honestly say northern Wales still remains my favourite place to go birdwatching.

The island of Anglesey offers everything, from towering sea cliffs thronged with seabird colonies, coastal heaths with choughs, estuaries teaming with waders and wildfowl, lakes and rivers, and every type of woodland you can think of! All this fantastic habitat is squeezed onto a compact island with good infrastructure to make so many sites easily accessible – if you know just where to look!

I have worked for the RSPB as Reserve Manager at the Conwy Nature Reserve and run Birdline Wales, the telephone information service. I have been privileged not only to visit all these sites, but to help many others find out about them, and which birds they can expect to see there. Now Ruth's book can spread the word about all our marvellous birdwatching sites to a new and wider audience. I am sure that you will enjoy discovering the walks and take great pleasure from the birds, wildlife, views and places that you see along the way. I shall certainly keep a copy with me on my birding travels around Anglesey, so I will be able to find the best spot for a warming cuppa and a bite to eat!

Alan Davies
former Reserve Manager, Conwy RSPB; Birdline Wales;
freelance Bird Guide

Remember ...

Before you go, tell someone where you're going.

Even if you take a mobile phone with you, there might not be good reception all the way. (But please, keep it switched off, or in 'silent' mode!)

Read the walk description carefully before leaving, and make sure you're wearing the right footwear; it's always a good idea to take waterproofs in a rucksack – in Wales, the weather can change very suddenly.

THE COUNTRY CODE
- Guard against any risk of fire.
- Keep to public rights of way when crossing farmland.
- Avoid causing any damage to walls, fences and hedges.
- Leave farm gates as you find them.
- Keep dogs under control and on leads in the presence of livestock.
- Leave machinery, farm animals and crops alone.
- Take care not to pollute water.
- Carry your litter home with you.
- Protect all wildlife, plants and trees.
- Avoid making any unnecessary noise.
- Drive carefully on country roads.
- Enjoy and respect the countryside.

Map of Anglesey with list of walks

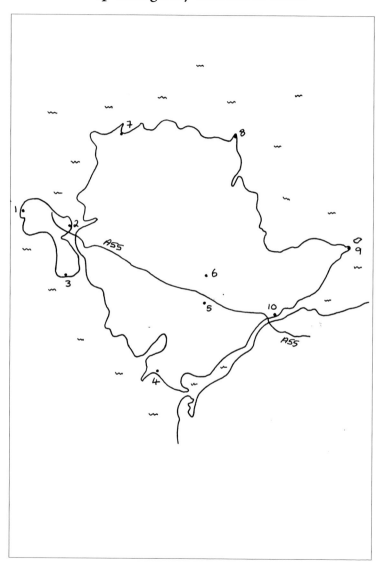

1. South Stack RSPB Reserve
2. Beddmanarch Bay/Penrhos Coastal Park
3. Rhoscolyn
4. Newborough Forest/Llanddwyn
5. Malltraeth RSPB Reserve
6. Cefni Reservoir and The Dingle, Llangefni
7. Cemlyn Bay
8. Point Lynas
9. Penmon
10. Church Island/Menai Bridge

South Stack RSPB Reserve

Site highlights:
- Excellent views of breeding seabird colony
- RSPB visitor centre in spring/summer to help you make the most of your visit
- **THE** place in northern Wales to visit to see Puffins in early summer, and Choughs all year round
- Beautiful coastline with stunning views, heathland and wild flowers

Map and grid reference:
OS Map 114 (Anglesey/Môn), SH 210 819

Site directions:
Follow the A55 North Wales Expressway all the way to Holyhead, Anglesey. As you enter Holyhead, at a set of traffic lights, you will leave the A55 which heads towards the ferry terminal. Continue forwards on the A5154 towards the town of Holyhead. Continue on this road until you reach the end of the public road; beyond this point it becomes the container terminal. Turn left, keeping the harbour and coastguard station on your right. At a mini-roundabout, turn left into a residential road. Continue along this until you reach a T-junction at the end. Turn right, and continue along this road as it passes through a residential area until you reach open countryside. About 1½ miles/2.4 km after you leave the town, a narrow lane heads off to your right, with a brown sign for South Stack RSPB. Drive up this narrow lane carefully, looking out for other drivers, pedestrians and, of course, birds. After just over ½ mile/0.8 km, you will reach a free RSPB car park off to your left where you should park and start your walk. This is a popular destination,

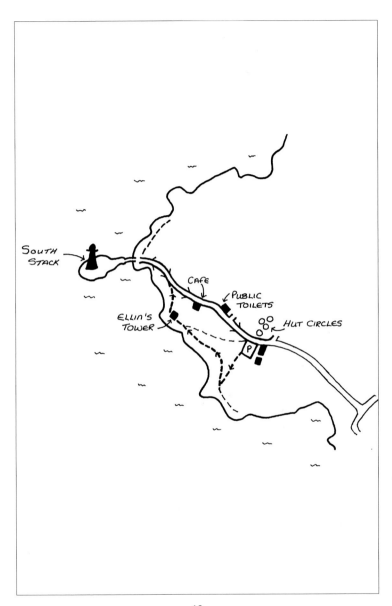

SOUTH STACK

CAFE

PUBLIC TOILETS

ELLIN'S TOWER

HUT CIRCLES

P

13

particularly in summer, so it may be better to arrive early in the morning.

Headline description

South Stack is the most north-westerly point of the north-westerly corner of Anglesey, and is in fact on Holy Island, an island off an island. Keep heading north-west and your next stop is Ireland, a point that migrating birds are well aware of. This is a stunning piece of coastline, and seen in summer the colours of the heather, gorse and wildflowers are a real joy. However, if it's a bird spectacle that you're after, then visit in late spring/early summer to enjoy the amazing sight, sound and smell of the breeding seabird colony. The sheer numbers of Razorbills, Guillemots and Fulmars packed tightly onto vertiginous ledges, and the to-ing and fro-ing of adult birds raising their chicks here has to be seen to be believed, and of course, this is THE place to look for Puffins in the early summer months. But don't forget to visit at other times of year too. This is on a key migration route in spring and autumn and the area has a good record for attracting rarities. And you can marvel at the aerial acrobatics of Choughs and Ravens at any time of year, while the fresh breezes blow the cobwebs away!

Length of walk:
Approximately 1 hour (1 mile/1.6 km)

Type of terrain:
The coastal path, which gives the best views, is narrow, rocky and steep in places, and can be slippery in wet conditions, so sturdy walking shoes are recommended.

Alternatively, there is a level path giving wheelchair access from the car park to a viewing area by Ellin's Tower.

Puffin

Walk directions:
Your birdwatching may have begun even before you reach the car park! Driving along slowly with the window open, you may hear Choughs calling nearby before you see them, either tumbling in the sky or alternatively landed in the fields on either side of the road. You may see them busily probing the ground with their distinctive curved red bills, as they are searching for insects. Leatherjacket larvae are a particular Chough favourite, and the fields under RSPB ownership around here are grazed by cattle to create the perfect conditions. Wales has around half the UK Chough population, and the reserve area holds around 4% of the Welsh birds, so this area is of great importance to Choughs.

The fields either side of the narrow lane up to South Stack are also the best place to look for the Hooded Crow that has been resident here for a few years now – but beware! She has bred with Carrion Crows during this time to give rise to a number of hybrid birds, ready to trap the unwary birdwatcher. These hybrids will show the same pattern of lighter grey body with dark head, breast, wings and tail, but once you see the real McCoy, you will appreciate the contrast of the significantly paler body of the full-blooded Hooded Crow.

Having parked in the RSPB car park, follow the footpath which leads straight out towards the cliffs.

As you walk between the heather and gorse, look out for Stonechats, Meadow Pipits and Wrens calling from the tops of bushes. In summer, the sky overhead may be filled with the beautiful songs of Skylarks. In 2004, this area attracted a rare Black Lark, more usually found on the steppes of Mongolia! This bird, a first for Britain, in turn attracted around five thousand birders during the eight days it stayed here, so keep your eyes peeled, as anything could turn up here.

At the 'Dangerous Cliffs' sign, turn right and follow the path towards Ellin's Tower.

There is plenty to look out for all around you but the sign is quite accurate: there is a long drop onto some very sharp rocks below, so do not forget where you are as you enjoy the wildlife! You are very likely to see Ravens enjoying the thermals along the cliff edge: these aerial acrobats are a pleasure to watch as they tumble, turn and even fly upside-down! Choughs may also be flying overhead, in pairs in spring, or in small family groups in winter if the young have not yet moved on to their own territories. Peer (carefully!) down at the water below you, and you are likely to see auks such as Razorbills and Guillemots bobbing about on the water. Further out to sea, seabirds may be passing: Gannets, Cormorants, Shags, Kittiwakes and Manx Shearwaters may all be heading up or down the coast between feeding and roosting areas. In spring and summer, the wildflowers at your feet are worth a closer look too: Kidney

Vetch, Squill, Thrift, Sheep's-bit add jewel-like colour to the scene.

Continue along the footpath for about ¹/₄ mile/0.4 km until you reach Ellin's Tower.

This is a Grade 2 listed folly, which now acts as the RSPB Visitor Centre for the site. From Easter to September it is open daily from 10 am to 5.30 pm and can be accessed via a steep flight of stairs. Inside you will find information on the plant, animal and bird life around you, and volunteers on hand with their telescopes to point out specific species of interest. From here, if you arrive in Spring and early Summer, you will be able to enjoy the fantastic spectacle of the seabird city on the cliffs opposite, but don't worry if the tower isn't open, there is an excellent viewing area just beside it.

This bird assault on the senses has to be seen to be believed, as thousands of birds are crammed together at this breeding site. On every narrow horizontal ledge, Razorbills and Guillemots jostle for position to lay an egg and raise their young; no room for a nest, the egg is laid directly on the ledge but is shaped with a particularly pointed end, so it will roll in a tight circle rather than fall off the ledge. Higher up on the cliffs, Fulmars and occasional Herring Gulls are also nesting. There is a constant flow of birds heading out to sea and returning with fish for the brooding adult and the growing young – how do they find their way back to the right partner?! Quietly watching all this activity, you may spot a Peregrine lurking, biding its time to catch out an unsuspecting bird. The noise and smell of this spectacle is incredible, and should not be missed, so aim to visit between late April and late June!

Everyone loves Puffins, and this is one of the best places in Wales to see these comedy birds. They also come to South Stack to breed, so late April to August is the best time to look for them here. You are unlikely to see them in great numbers, but study

Ellin's Tower and South Stack Lighthouse

the birds on the water carefully, and you should see one or two, the orange feet paddling away behind are a give-away! Alternatively you may see them on the rocks closer to the water level.

The cliffs here are popular with rock climbers, so do not be surprised if you see people, suitably harnessed and hard-hatted, disappearing over the edge! However, an agreement has been arranged which maintains a 'closed season' in spring for climbing, to ensure the birds breeding on the cliffs are not disturbed.

If rare plants are your thing, this is the only place in the world you can see the Spatulate Fleawort. The RSPB volunteers should be able to point out this unassuming but endemic plant on the cliff edge opposite the breeding colony.

From Ellin's Tower, continue along the footpath by the cliff, and climb the steep stone steps up to the road level.

Scan the water again while catching your breath. You may see more Choughs overhead, and are likely to see seabirds rounding the headland further out to see. If the sea is not too choppy, you may spot a Harbour Porpoise in the water. Looking to your right, you have a good view of South Stack Lighthouse.

If you wish to visit the lighthouse, walk to the end of the road. It is open from early April onwards, and is managed by Trinity House. Tickets can be bought at the lighthouse itself or the café at South Stack. Visitors can look over the former engine room and exhibition before climbing the lighthouse tower itself. The lighthouse is actually on a small island separate from the mainland, and at one time, visitors to the island had to pass across in a basket hauled along a rope. Nowadays there is a bridge, though you still have to descend four hundred steps down the cliff. Of course this means there are four hundred steps back up again!

If you don't wish to explore the lighthouse, walk back down the road towards the car park. You will shortly pass the South Stack Kitchen. This café serves hot and cold drinks, snacks and ice creams and is open in high season only.

Continue back down the road to the car park, passing some public toilets on your left on the way.

As you reach the entrance to the car park, you will notice a sign pointing to the Hut Circles on your left. This is quite an extensive site, containing the remains of some fifty buildings. The site was in use from the Iron Age (500 BC) until to Roman times, though all the buildings are unlikely to have been used continuously during this period. The site was first excavated in the 1860s, though more buildings were uncovered in the 1970s. There appear to be eight homesteads with a variety of storage buildings and workshops attached to the dwellings. The buildings were round with low stone walls upon which roof timbers would have rested to support a thatch or turf roof. The occupants appear to have been farmers, keeping livestock and growing a few crops, while also gathering some food from the sea shore.

What to look for …

… in spring: Stonechats, Linnets and Wrens are likely to be calling from the tops of gorse bushes, while Skylarks will be starting to sing overhead. You may even be lucky enough to see a rarity such as a Hoopoe, Bluethroat or Wryneck: these have in the past been seen here at this time. In late spring, the wildflowers will also be starting to bloom along the cliff edges, and this is the best time to look for the South Stack-endemic Spatulate Fleawort!

… in spring/summer: This is the time to view the breeding colony: Razorbills, Guillemonts, Fulmars, Herring Gulls and Puffins should all be nesting in the area. Keep an eye open for Peregrines on the look-out for an easy meal. You may also see the rare Silver-studded Blue Butterfly on the shorter heathland.

… in autumn: In autumn, this is a good place to look for migrants as they head westwards towards Ireland. Pick a calm day and arrive early in the morning and you should be able to see thrushes, starlings, larks, finches and buntings passing through. Bring your telescope as it is a great location for sea-watching. Rarities turn up here in Autumn too: Red-breasted Flycatcher, Pallas' Warbler and Grey Catbird, a first for Britain, have all been seen here.

 … all year round: This is one of the best places in Wales to see Choughs in good numbers and you should hear and see them all year round. You should also be rewarded with good views of Ravens at any time of year along the cliff line, and Peregrines are seen overhead regularly too. Check the heathland, the small fields and areas of cover for smaller birds. Stonechats and Rock Pipits by the cliffs are regulars too, and of course the Hooded Crow is around all year.

Where to eat:
South Stack Kitchen is not part of the RSPB reserve but is privately owned. It is open in high season and offers hot and cold drinks and meals, snacks, and ices. The café car park at the top of the hill is available for café users and visitors to the lighthouse only. Call 01407 762181 for details of opening hours.

Other information:
- Free RSPB car park open all year round
- Public Toilets available all year
- RSPB Visitor Centre in Ellin's Tower open Easter to September

South Stack Lighthouse

What other sights are nearby:
- The Range (car park at SH 211 818) is another headland just south of South Stack, owned by the RSPB. This area of heathland is a good spot for sea-watching: take your telescope out to the point and settle down for a good display of passing seabirds
- Breakwater Country Park, Holyhead
- Penrhos Coastal Park and café (weekdays only) at Beddmanarch Bay, Holyhead
- Trearddur Bay

Beddmanarch Bay/Penrhos Coastal Park

Site highlights:
- Easy walking in attractive coastal scenery
- Mix of estuarine and woodland walking and birding

Map and grid reference:
OS Map 114 (Anglesey/Môn), SH 275 805

Site directions:
Leave the A55 at the Valley exit. Take the A5 north towards Valley, and at the traffic lights, continue straight ahead through Valley. Drive across the Stanley Embankment with Beddmanarch Bay on your right, and at the end of the embankment, take the first turning on the right by the toll house for Penrhos Coastal Park. Drive down the narrow lane and park in the car park overlooking the bay.

Headline description
This is an easy circular walk offering attractive views across the bay and a variety of habitat from coastal to woodland. As a result you can enjoy a variety of birdlife too, from waders and gulls in Beddmanarch Bay, to woodland birds and summer migrants in the grounds of the former grand estate here. Although the car park at Penrhos Coast Park may be busy, a short walk down the path will soon take you away from the crowds and you can enjoy the peaceful scenery by yourself.

Length of walk:
Approximately $2^{1}/_{2}$ hours ($3^{1}/_{2}$ miles/5.6 km)

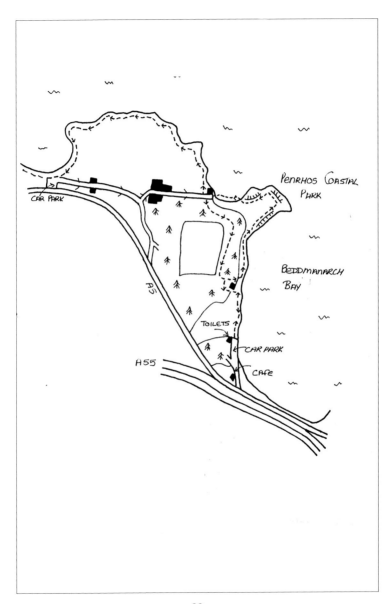

PENRHOS COASTAL PARK

BEDDMANARCH BAY

CAR PARK

A5

A55

TOILETS

CAR PARK

CAFE

23

Type of terrain:
Sandy beach, metalled lane and grassy paths on the headland and through the woods; can become muddy in places.

Walk directions:
Before heading off on your walk, take time to scan the bay, ideally with a telescope. This is the widest part of the waterway that technically separates Holy Island from the rest of Anglesey. The shallows here mean that the tide advances and retreats a long way, and rapidly, here. At low tide, the mudflats are exposed and you should see a good range of waders including Oystercatchers, Ringed Plovers, Curlews, and in season, Whimbrels, Bar-tailed and Black-tailed Godwits. Pale-bellied Brent Geese often congregate here in winter, and it is always worth checking the gull flocks to see if you can pick out something unusual amongst the Common, Herring, and Black-headed regulars. Look further out across the water with your telescope in winter, and you may be rewarded with Great Northern Divers and Slavonian Grebes, as well as the more regular Great Crested Grebes, Cormorants and Red-breasted Mergansers.

From the car park, take the metalled path past the toilet block on your left, and continue onwards keeping the bay on your right until you reach Beddmanarch House after about ¼ mile/0.4 km. The path turns inland here to circuit the house and you need to turn right past a wooden gate. You shortly reach the site of a Pet Cemetery, where you turn right following the Anglesey Coastal Path until you are back at the shore again. Turn left and walk past the bench and shelter. A bit further along, you will pass 'Tunnicliffe's Seat' on your right. On reaching a patch of open grass, you may wish to check the small pond on your left for duck and Grey Heron, while, in summer, warblers may be lurking in the surrounding bushes. Just past this point the path splits. Take the right hand path, still following the

Anglesey Coastal Path, which leads you out into an open area of traditionally-managed meadowland. Walk to the top of the hill and enjoy the views from the top of Gorsedd-y-penrhyn of Beddmanarch Bay to your right, and Holyhead Harbour and Holyhead Mountain in the distance to your left. A thoughtfully-placed stone seat means you can admire the view in either direction.

Butterflies such as Clouded Yellow, Tortoiseshell, and Peacock are attracted in summer to the wildflowers in this area of unspoiled

Spring at Penrhos Coastal Park

meadowland which is managed by Anglesey Aluminium who bought the Penrhos Estate in 1972. Check the bushes all around this area for summer migrants: Lesser and Common Whitethroats can be found here, Blackcaps, Garden Warblers and Grasshopper Warblers can be heard (if not seen) here too. Scanning across towards the Alaw estuary, you may be able to add to your list of waders, while you may see Cormorants and terns flying past the point as you look out to sea. Facing towards Holyhead Harbour, you may see in the distance one of the ferries or the catamaran that crosses to Ireland from here.

From here, head back down the other side of the flower meadow and take the small path on the right down on to the beach. Turn left and follow the sandy beach round towards the white house, following the footpath back up into the trees by the red lifebelt, just before you reach the house.

The area of Penrhos Coastal Path was the estate of the Stanley family from 1763. Apparently this area used to be their private beach, and in later years the building here served as a 'beach hut'.

Walk past a wooden gate and along the lane for a very short distance before taking the footpath on your right, signposted the Anglesey Coastal Path. Follow this path for about ¾ mile/1.2 km as it winds its way along the cliff, past the ruins of what used to be a boathouse, and the 'The Battery'.

Ahead of you is the smelting works of Anglesey Aluminium Metal Ltd, whose chimney which can be seen for miles around. It is one of the largest employers in northern Wales, employing over five hundred staff, and produces some 142,000 tonnes of aluminium a year. It takes most of its power from Wylfa Power Station on north Anglesey near Cemlyn Lagoon.

Follow the yellow footpath markers as the path descends through the dunes towards a car park. As you reach the lane, turn left and walk past some houses. At the junction, continue straight ahead through the stone gateway towards Penrhos Farm, following the blue footpath marker. Pass the cricket pitch on your left (keeping an eye out for Mistle Thrushes and Pied Wagtails strutting about on its tended lawn) and continue towards the farm. When you reach the buildings, bear left towards Penrhos Farm, passing 'The Tower' on your right and keeping the cricket pitch on your left, following the blue footpath marker. Pass a square tower on your left and walk straight across an open yard, keeping some old buildings on your right. Go through a wooden gate marked 'Beach House' and walk down the lane still following the blue footpath marker. You will soon reach the white house again, but this time, turn right to pass into the woods through the gate in the stone wall.

These woods are a real joy in May, when the leaves are still in their bright green colouring, and the floor is carpeted with bluebells and wild garlic. The scent is heavenly as you walk along, and the trees are not leaved so thickly that you cannot, with some persistence, see the birds that are singing around you: Chiffchaffs, Willow Warblers, Garden Warblers, Blackcaps, Song Thrushes, Blackbirds, Robins and Wrens. As well as wildlife, these woodlands are reputed to be home to a number of ghosts too: one, who has been seen by a number of people is that of a German parachutist who is supposed to have bailed out of his damaged aircraft only to be killed upon landing in the woods. There are no historical records to support this story, but nevertheless, keep your eyes peeled for an unusual sight in the trees!

Turn right by the footpath sign to walk towards an ornamental column. Continue past this straight ahead to walk through a gap in the high wall.

The old walls and stone steps that you can just make out here suggest that this was once part of a more formal garden. Some rhododendrons and spotted laurels grow here, and in May the air is heady with the scent of the wild garlic at your feet.

Turn left at a yellow footpath marker just before a bench and take the right fork past a stone wall. The footpath takes a meandering route to bring you back through a gap in the high wall out onto a wider path. Turn right here and walk through a tunnel of trees. Turn left by a yellow footpath marker at the corner of a stone wall on your left, and walk past the ruins of some mini 'ramparts'. Keeping the stone wall on your left, continue straight ahead at a crossroads of footpaths. At the next crossroads amongst some conifer trees, continue straight ahead again, listening carefully for any Coal Tits or Goldfinches in the area. Crossing a wooden bridge over a stream, you reach the pet cemetery once again. Turn right, pass a wooden gate and then turn left to get back to the water's edge and your route back to the car park.

If birds or wild flowers tempt you to wander down alternative paths through the woodland, don't worry. There are many paths to take here, and providing you keep the slight traffic noise from the main road on your right, you can't go far wrong.

Dunlin flock

What to look for …

… in spring: Pale-bellied Brent Geese and Slavonian Grebes may be seen out on the water up until the end of April, by which time the Grebes may be looking particularly fine in their breeding plumage, as well as Great Northern Divers. Look out also for passage waders such as Bar-tailed Godwits and Whimbrels, Dunlins, Knots and Sanderlings. In late spring and summer, the woodland and parkland areas are likely to be resounding with the songs of warblers such as Willow Warblers, Chiffchaffs, Common and Lesser Whitethroats, reeling Grasshopper Warblers, and who knows, maybe a rarity might drop in.

… in summer: Look offshore when you're walking along the coastal cliffs for terns, usually Common or Sandwich Terns, but if you're lucky, you may also catch sight of an Arctic Tern. Keep checking the woodland and hedgerow areas in early summer for warblers, as well as woodland regulars such as mixed tit flocks.

… in autumn: Passage waders are likely to be passing through again, using the exposed mudflats of the bay as a stopping off point. Look out for Bar-tailed Godwits, Knots, Whimbrels, Sanderlings, Dunlins and Grey Plovers.

… in winter: Brent Geese will be returning to the bay again, as will Slavonian and Great Crested Grebes and Great Northern Divers. Bar-tailed Godwits, Knots, Dunlins and Grey Plovers may also still be here, particularly outside high tide. In cold weather, this can be a good place to do your birdwatching from the warmth and comfort from your car in the car park.

 … all year round: You should be able to see a variety of gulls, Red-breasted Mergansers, and waders such as Oystercatchers, Ringed Plovers, Cormorants and Curlews here all year round, particularly when the tide is falling and the mudflats are exposed.

Where to eat:
The Toll House is situated at the entrance to the car park of Penrhos Coast Park. This was set up as a café to offer supported employment for people with learning disabilities and was open to the public from August 1988. However, it closed in November 2008 pending a feasibility study and had not reopened at the time of going to print. Call 01407 760247 to see if it has reopened.

The Toll House itself has an interesting history. As the Stanley Tollhouse, it was originally located next to the Telford Road at the Holyhead end of the embankment. However, in the 1960s it had to be moved by Anglesey County Council to make way for a water main in connection with the Anglesey Aluminium smelting plant up the road. The entire tollhouse was dismantled stone by stone and rebuilt slightly further down the road in its present position. Each side of the building was painted in two different colours and each stone numbered in sequence to ensure it was all put back together again in the right order!

Alternative cafés can be found at the village of Valley, just five minutes away by car, down the A5 heading south towards the A55. At the traffic lights, turn right and park in the car park on the left. There are a couple of good cafés here: Caffi Arian on the main Station Road, and Café Milano off the car park itself.

Other information:
- Free car park
- Public toilets on site

What other sights are nearby:
- Holyhead Harbour, and Breakwater Country Park
- South Stack RSPB Reserve
- Anglesey Coastal Path

Fishing boats at Holyhead harbour

Rhoscolyn

Site highlights:
- Dramatic coastal scenery of cliffs, sea arches, narrow coves and sandy beaches
- Chance to see Choughs and Ravens tumbling over the cliffs, as well as sea-watching for gulls, auks and Manx Shearwaters
- Magnificent views ranging from Holyhead Mountain on Anglesey to Eryri/Snowdonia

Map and grid reference:
OS Map 114 (Anglesey/Môn), SH 272 751

Site directions:
From the A55, take the A5 exit for Valley and Trearddur (not RAF Valley) and follow the A5 for 3/4 mile/1.2 km to Valley. At the traffic lights, turn left onto the B4545 towards Trearddur Bay. Cross over the level crossing and bridge over the A55. At the small roundabout, continue straight on the B4545. After about a mile/1.6 km, you cross Four Mile Bridge with the 'inland sea' on both sides of you. After about 1/4 mile/0.4 km, take the minor road to your left, signposted Rhoscolyn. Follow this lane for about 2 miles/3.2 km to Rhoscolyn village, ignoring a left turn to Silver Bay. By the public house, turn left signposted to the beach. This is a single track lane with many sharp turns so proceed with caution. At the end is a small car park. Space is limited and the car park can quickly fill at peak times, so you may want to aim for an early morning walk here!

Headline description
This walk gives you the opportunity to include one of the more

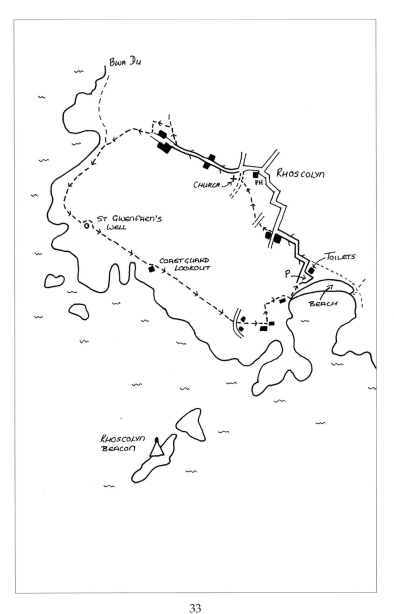

Bwa Du

Rhoscolyn

Church
PH

St Gwenfaen's Well

Coastguard Lookout

Toilets

P

Beach

Rhoscolyn Beacon

spectacular sections of the Anglesey Coastal Path, with its sudden indentations concealing narrow coves, dramatic sea arches undermined by the waves, and sheltered sandy bays. Although the inclines you cover are gentle, the slight rise gives you fantastic panoramic views across Anglesey as well as towards Eryri/Snowdonia and the hills of Yr Eifl on the Llŷn. The fantastic view from the Coastguard Lookout makes you appreciate the reefs and rocks of this dramatic coastline, and the hazards it has presented to shipping over the years. A walk along this coastline may give you good views of the charismatic Chough and Raven, while sea-watching may reward you with views of Manx Shearwaters and auks.

Length of walk:
Approximately 2 hours (3^1/$_2$ miles/5.6 km)

Type of terrain:
A mixture of lanes, tracks and grassy and stony paths; walking footwear recommended.

Walk directions:
Leave the car park and walk back up the lane along which you have driven, for ^{1}/$_4$ mile/0.4 km. At a sharp right hand bend, go through the metal gate by a footpath sign beside a house. Follow the footpath between a hedge and the wall. Go through the gate and follow the right-hand side of the field.

You will notice that all the bushes and small trees have a definite slant, a clear indication of the prevailing wind direction!

Go through the kissing gate, and continue straight across the narrow part of the field to the next kissing gate. Walk diagonally across the next field heading for the corner of the wall. Climb the ladder stile, with the church in front of you. Head for the gate to your right, at the end of the track. Turn left

Chough

into the lane and immediately left again on the road past the church.

There has been a church on this site since AD 630, though the current Church of St Gwenfaen dates from 1871. The archway protected inside the porch is fifteenth century.

Ignore a footpath sign to your left by the corner of the cemetery and continue on the lane past some cottages as the lane becomes a rough track.

To your right, you have good views of Anglesey Aluminium Plant, and the rather more attractive coastline of Trearddur Bay. In the background is Holyhead Mountain (*Mynydd y Tŵr*), and you can just see Ellin's Tower on the RSPB reserve of South Stack to its left.

Just before you reach the farm, follow the footpath signs to bear right round the farmyard. Go through two kissing gates, and bear left towards the next yellow footpath markers. At the corner, turn left to rejoin the track going right. Pass through another kissing gate and follow the path between broken stone walls, heading for yet another kissing gate. At this point you join the Anglesey Coastal Path.

The Anglesey Coastal Path has recently opened in its new guise as a 125-mile long path circumnavigating the whole island. Stretches of coastal path have existed for many years, but it is only recently that there has been the will and the funding to turn the concept of a circular walk into reality. New signposts clearly mark the course of the Coastal Path, which, with a few exceptions, follows the coastline quite closely. Work has been carried out in places to create a sturdy stone path to protect the underlying soil from erosion. The entire walk can be completed in five to six days if you are a fast walker. However, it is probably more realistic to take your time, not least to allow for the tides which may rise to cover certain sections of the coastal path for a few hours either side of high tide.

The path here brings you out at a narrow cove. You may wish to make a small detour along the Coastal Path to your right here to see the dramatic cliff formation and sea arch of Bwa Du and Bwa Gwyn, where the sea has gradually eroded the softer rock

Sheltered cove near Rhoscolyn

underneath, leaving a narrow arch out over the water.

Notice the particular pink strata in the cliff face here. If you look closely, you may notice Rock Pipits and Turnstones fossicking about amongst the stones on the beach while Choughs and Ravens enjoy the thermal uplift along the cliff edges. Both birds have distinctive calls which carry on the wind long before you may be able to see them. As you walk back along the coastline, keep an eye out to sea for passing seabirds such as gulls, auks such as Razorbills and Guillemots, and Manx Shearwaters.

Turn left and follow the Coastal Path, keeping the wall to your left and taking care where the path is close to the cliff edge.

It may be worth checking the fields to your left for more Choughs. You pass a stone enclosure of St Gwenfaen's Well. This was a place of pilgrimage in the Middle Ages, as its waters were believed to have healing properties.

The path aims towards the Coastguard Lookout, which is no longer in use but provides an excellent viewpoint.

To your right you can look back across the bays and reefs of the western shore of Anglesey towards South Stack and Holyhead Mountain further round, while to your left, if the weather is fine, you can see as far as the mountains of Eryri/Snowdonia and Yr Eifl hills on the mainland. Directly in front of you lies the Rhoscolyn Beacon on its own separate rocky island. Keep an eye out for Peregrines and Kestrels which may nest on the cliffs here.

Leaving the Coastguard Lookout behind you, follow the Coastal Path downhill, ignoring a track off to the left. Go through a kissing gate and walk straight across the field to the next one.

The stone walls and thistle-rich fields in this area attract Stonechats, Linnets and Goldfinches and flocks of juvenile Starlings in good numbers in early autumn.

Follow the footpath signs between buildings, then turn to your left and continue on a path between stone walls. Continue on the narrow path between houses and go straight ahead across a lawn. Walk down the driveway towards the small bay, and then bear left following the Coastal Path sign. Cross the beach to return to the car park. If the tide is in, you can chance your walk across the beach between the waves or, if you prefer, go up the steps to your left and follow the safety of the path behind the sea wall.

What to look for ...

... in spring/summer: In the hedgerows and fields along your way you are very likely to come across Linnets, and in the more open grassy areas, you should hear Skylarks singing high above you. Looking out to sea, you may see birds flying over the water such as Manx Shearwaters, Gannets, Razorbills, Guillemots, Fulmars, and Kittiwakes, though you are likely to need a telescope for good views.

... in autumn: Passage waders are likely to be passing through again, using the exposed mudflats of the bay as a stopping off point. Look out for Bar-tailed Godwits, Knots, Whimbrels, Sanderlings, Dunlins and Grey Plovers.

... in winter: In the fields along your walk you are likely to see patches of thistle, a particularly good place to look in autumn for Goldfinches.

... all year round: Anywhere near the coastal cliffs around here you are likely to see and hear Choughs and Ravens. Both have distinctive calls which carry on the wind, and both are birds which take full advantage of the air currents to tumble, swoop and dive in the air. Kestrels should be seen, hovering motionless in the wind as they search for small rodents on the ground, while Peregrines may flash past you on the search for prey. Check the tops of gorse or heather and likely fence posts for Stonechats. In grassy areas you are very likely to come across Meadow Pipits, which rise up suddenly from the grass at your approach. Their slightly darker cousins, Rock Pipits, are very likely to be seen at the very cliff edges or hopping around the rocks at the edge of the bay at Rhoscolyn. Turnstones are also likely here at the water's edge, while looking down onto the rocks at the foot of the cliffs and in the sea around you may see Cormorants or Shags.

Where to eat:
The café Y Gegin Fach (*the small kitchen*) at Four Mile Bridge offers very reasonably priced drinks, cakes and hot and cold snacks. It is open all year until 4.30 p.m. (last orders for hot food 4 p.m.), but closed on Mondays. To reach it from the car park, retrace your route on the minor roads to the B4545. Y Gegin Fach is opposite the junction where the minor road joins the B Road.

Other information:
- Free car park, though space is very limited. Aim to arrive early at peak times to be sure of a parking space
- Public toilets in the car park
- Boats can be launched from the bay for a fee

What other sights are nearby:
- South Stack RSPB Reserve
- Four Mile Bridge and the 'inland sea', a usually windy but often productive spot for birding
- Valley Lakes nature reserve with wildfowl below and RAF jets above
- Newborough Forest and Newborough Warren for pine forests, sand dunes and shoreline

Newborough Forest and Ynys Llanddwyn

Site highlights:
- Fantastic mixture of wide sandy beaches, sheltered rocky coves, sand dunes and pine forests
- Stunning views across to Eryri/Snowdonia and Yr Eifl on the Llŷn peninsula
- Shore birds all year round and pine forest species
- Historic buildings and church ruins on Ynys (*island*) Llanddwyn

Map and grid reference:
OS Map 114 (Anglesey/Môn), SH 406 635

Site directions:
On the A55 heading west, cross over the Britannia Bridge and take the next exit, turning left onto the A5 towards Llanfair Pwllgwyngyll. After ³/₄ mile/1.2 km, turn left onto the A4080 towards Brynsiencyn. Continue on this road for approximately 11 miles/17.7 km until you reach the village of Newborough. Take the first turning left in the centre of the village and continue on this lane for just over a mile/1.6 km until you reach the toll barrier at the entrance to Newborough Forest, where a fee is payable. Continue along this lane to the large car park at the end, ignoring a right turn and another car park about halfway along.

Headline description
This is an exhilarating place to walk along the stunning wide open beach with a backdrop of the Eryri/Snowdonian mountains and Yr Eifl in the distance, and the island of Llanddwyn, shrouded in legend, as your destination. En route

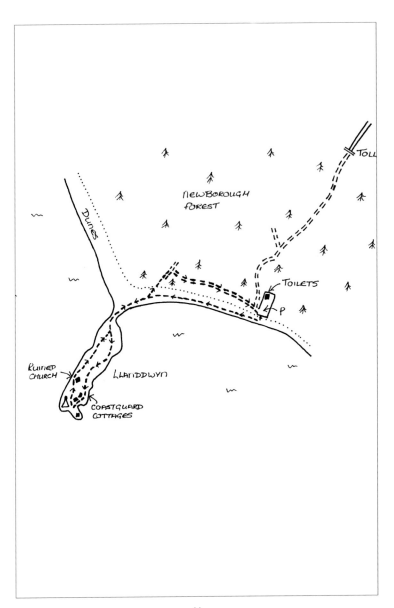

TOLL

NEWBOROUGH
FOREST

Dunes

TOILETS

P

RUINED
CHURCH

LLANDDWYN

COASTGUARD
COTTAGES

41

you can enjoy shore birds busy at the water's edge, Cormorants and Shags massing on the rocks, and sea birds passing in the distance. On the return journey, the constant crash of waves is muffled amongst the pine trees, where the high pitched calls of Goldcrests and Crossbills may catch your ear, and who knows, you may even catch a glimpse of an elusive Red Squirrel.

Length of walk:
Approximately $2^1/_2$ hours (4 miles/6.4 km)

Type of terrain:
Shingle beach, grassy paths and forest tracks. Comfortable footwear recommended.

Walk directions:
From the car park, head towards the beach, taking the right hand fork in the path through the dunes out onto the beach. You will immediately enjoy stunning views, with Yr Wyddfa/Snowdon and Yr Eifl on the Llŷn to your left, and Llanddwyn Island to your right. Turn right and walk along the beach with the dunes and forest on your right.

Look out for birds on the shoreline including Oystercatchers, gulls and, outside the summer months, Sanderlings. Stonechats breed here and may be seen at any time of year on the rocks and bushes. Look up, and you are likely to see a Buzzard or Raven flying over the forest and sand dunes.

When you reach Llanddwyn, a sand bar connects the slightly higher land on the island with the mainland. This spit of land becomes narrower at high tide, but don't worry. It is generally only covered completely by water at exceptionally high spring tides so you are unlikely to get cut off!

Llanddwyn is named after Wales' patron saint of lovers, the

Lighthouse on Llanddwyn

maiden Dwynwen, who lived here in the fifth century. According to the legend, Dwynwen fell in love with Prince Maelon when he visited the island, and he was so infatuated with her that he tried to seduce her. She resisted his advances and they parted in bitterness. Grieving Dwynwen was visited by an angel who gave her a potion to cure her of her love sickness and to wreak vengeance upon Maelon. Becoming a hermit, Dwynwen established a shrine on the island which was visited by many pilgrims seeking guidance and solace in matters of the heart. The story goes that with the aid of waters from her secret well, Dwynwen was able to divine whether a loved one was being faithful or not.

Taking the track beside the information board, walk through the grass covered dunes towards the southern tip of the island. Please make sure that you keep to the clear footpaths in this protected area.

You will pass some restored pilots' cottages on your way, two of which are often open to the public and give a snapshot of life for the pilots and their families in the 1800s. The pilots manned the lighthouse and guided vessels into Caernarfon harbour, as well as acting as lifeboat men. The cannon in front of the cottages was used to summon the lifeboat crews in times of distress.

Walk to the end of the island and check the various sandy and rocky coves for wading birds, such as Oystercatchers and Ringed Plovers.

Large numbers of Cormorants often congregate on the rocks just offshore. In summer, it is worth scanning the sea for terns and Manx Shearwaters in summer, and divers in winter, and this can also be a very good place to see Grey Seals at any time of year. You are also likely to see Rock Pipits here on the rocks at the end of the island.

On the very point of the island are two white lighthouses. The smaller one to the left was built in 1819 and since 1972 has been used as the automatic beacon, while the larger one to the right was built in 1845 as a lighthouse but is now disused.

Follow the path which climbs up to the cross and follows the north-western coastline of the island back towards the mainland.

To your left you can look across Malltraeth Bay up the west coast of Anglesey to the beacon at Rhoscolyn, and in the distance you may see Holyhead Mountain (Mynydd Caergybi). To your right, on the island itself, you pass the ruins of a sixteenth-century church. This was built on the site of St Dwynwen's original church from the fifth century.

Descending some steps at the end of the island, you arrive again

Sanderling

at the sandbar. Cross this back to the mainland and turn right to walk back along the beach towards the car park. You can choose to complete your walk to the car park along the beach itself, returning via the footpath through the dunes. Alternatively, for a change of habitat and the opportunity to see more birds, you can return to your car through the woods. After walking a short distance along the beach, take a path up the bank into the forest. The going is easy along this wide forestry track through the pine trees.

This forest was planted in the 1950s to help stabilise the area of sand dunes which suffered from erosion and movement inland caused by the prevailing winds. The Corsican pine trees are well adapted to these sandy and salty conditions, and may harbour Coal Tits, Goldcrests, Great Spotted Woodpeckers and Common Crossbills. Historically this has been a significant site for roosting Ravens. There is also a small population of Red Squirrels here, though you would be extremely lucky to see one.

Ignore a second track to your left through the black and yellow barrier, as the main track you are following bends round to the right. After about half a mile/0.8 km, you will pass a disabled access trail with interpretation boards through an area of land developed to demontrate the type of vegetation typical of this habitat. Continue along the forest track for a further quarter of a mile/0.4 km to return to the public car park.

What to look for …

… in spring: Looking offshore you may see Sandwich Terns and Gannets passing. Turnstones may be seen along the water's edge in the rocky coves of the island and you may also see Sanderlings along the beach just ahead of the waves.

… in summer: Look out to see for Manx Shearwaters flying past out to sea, as well as Shags and auks on the water such as Razorbills and Guillemots. In the grassy areas of the island, you are likely to come across Meadow Pipits amongst the grasses and Skylarks singing overhead.

… in autumn: Look out for waders including Sanderlings, Knots, and Whimbrels along the shore. Look offshore for terns, Gannets and Manx Shearwaters and keep your eyes open for more interesting birds too; Arctic Skuas have been recorded from here.

… in winter: This is a good time of year to look offshore for divers such as Great Northern Divers and Slavonian Grebes, while Sanderlings may be along the shoreline.

… all year round: Look and listen out for Goldcrests, Coal Tits, Great Spotted Woodpeckers and Common Crossbills in all areas of pine forest. You are likely to see a Buzzard soaring overhead and this is a particularly good site to see Ravens. At any time of year you are likely to see Oystercatchers and Ringed Plovers at the water's edge along the beach and the rocky coves of the island. You should also see Rock Pipits at the end of the island too. Check the tops of gorse bushes and rocks for Stonechats.

Where to eat:
The White Lodge Café can be found at nearby Pen-lôn, just over five minutes' drive away. Return to the A4080 in Newborough and turn right. Continue about ¹/₂ mile/0.8 km until the roundabout and turn left. The White Lodge is immediately on your right by the caravan park, open 9 a.m. to 5 p.m. every day throughout the year and serves drinks, snacks, and hot and cold food.

Other information:
- Fee (£2 at time of going to print) payable to drive into Forestry Commission Land
- Public toilets and picnic tables in Forestry car park
- The sand bar to Llanddwyn may be covered by the sea at extreme high tides, but is passable at other times
- Please note dogs are only allowed on the beach in winter from 1st October to 30th March
- Please keep to marked footpaths through the protected habitat of the dunes

What other sights are nearby:
- Newborough Warren, an area of heathland, marshland and sand dunes
- Malltraeth cob and pool for waders and wildfowl
- Malltraeth RSPB Reserve
- Plas Newydd National Trust property and tearooms

Malltraeth RSPB Reserve

Site highlights:

- Footpaths out across Malltraeth Marsh/Cors Ddyga giving good views of wintering duck
- See Reed Buntings close up in reedbeds growing up to head-height
- Easy level there-and-back-again walk on gritted paths, or circular walk for the more intrepid

Map and grid reference:

OS Map 114 (Anglesey/Môn), SH 463 726

Site directions:

From the A55 Expressway in either direction, take the exit signposted for the A5 in the direction of Llangefni and Gaerwen. Follow the A5 towards Gaerwen which takes a sharp bend to the left and then continues in a straight line running parallel with the A55. After about a mile/1.6 km you cross the canalised afon/river Cefni. Slow down here as you will need to turn right very shortly. Immediately after the signs for Pentre Berw and the 40 mph speed limit, you need to turn right onto an unmarked and unmetalled track on the right hand side with a barn in the distance, which leads to the RSPB reserve of Malltraeth. (If you reach some buildings on the main road and start to go uphill, then you have missed the turning and will need to turn round.) Drive along this track for about ¼ mile/0.4 km, taking care as some of the potholes can be quite deep. You will reach a small cottage housing the RSPB reserve office; continue past this cottage and turn right at the T-junction of tracks, parking your car carefully in the small parking area here.

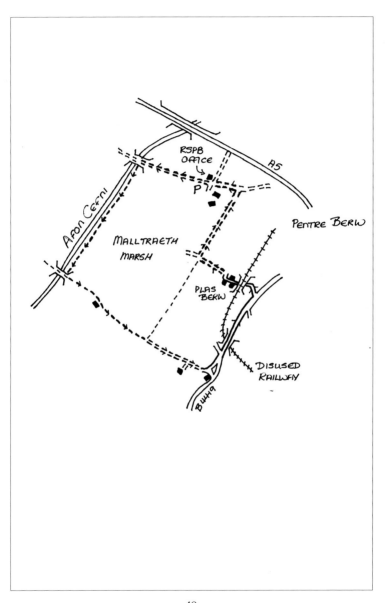

RSPB OFFICE

A5

Afon Cefni

Pentre Berw

MALLTRAETH MARSH

PLAS BERW

DISUSED RAILWAY

B4419

P

Headline description

This walk gives you a real sense of open space and big skies, almost reminiscent of East Anglia. As you walk alongside the canalised Afon Cefni, the path is well maintained and you can enjoy raised views across Malltraeth Marsh. Turn off onto the footpaths, however, and the habitat closes in around you. The track from this point on, which can at times be wet and muddy underfoot, leads you through reedbeds which grow to such a height they tower over you. Reed Buntings cling to the reeds at head-height, and you can peer through the rushes at duck meandering quietly on hidden pools. Hedgerow birds accompany you for the last stage of the walk, and you may be lucky enough to startle a Sparrowhawk on the prowl.

Length of walk:
Approximately 2 hours ($4^1/2$ miles/7.2 km)

Type of terrain:
Generally level terrain. Some of the paths are covered in slate chippings which make for very easy walking. However, in some places you will need to pick your way along muddy tracks, so Wellington boots are advisable for the full circular tour. Please note that at times animals may be grazing on the fields here. Graziers sometimes tie the gates shut to prevent their animals wandering, so you may have to climb over the odd five-barred gate. If you open any gates, please shut them firmly behind you.

Walk directions:
From the car park, continue westwards on foot down the track that leads off it for about a $^1/2$ mile/0.8 km towards the bridge over Afon Cefni.

Malltraeth Marsh is an SSSI (Site of Special Scientific Interest) managed by the RSPB, who are recreating 130 hectares of reedbeds with the aim of establishing Bitterns as a breeding

Marshy land at Malltraeth RSPB Reserve

species, and providing wet grassland as breeding habitat for Lapwing and other waders. Check the marshland on either side of the path here carefully. While you would be very lucky to see a Bittern, Lapwing are more commonly seen here in spring and summer. Reed Buntings, Stonechat and Linnets, often seen sitting up on the tops of scrub bushes, are resident species here. Snipe may be seen skulking around on the edge of the reeds. Duck such as Mallard, Gadwall and Shoveller are around all year, while Wigeon, Teal and Goldeneye are found here in winter. The elusive Garganey has been seen here on occasion in spring over a number of years.

Go through the metal gate and, just before you reach the grassy bridge, turn left along the footpath with Afon Cefni on your right and the dyke on your left.

This is a particularly good spot to look for Reed Buntings, who like to congregate on the reeds and fence posts here. In spring, Skylarks can also be seen on the ground, or as the season progresses, in the air in full song.

Continue along this path which runs in a straight line alongside the canalised river for about a mile/1.6 km until you reach the next bridge over the river.

As you walk along, check in the water channels that criss-cross these marshy fields for Grey Herons and Little Egrets fishing. Don't forget to keep your eyes peeled for raptors too: Common Buzzards may be perched in the trees surveying the scene, Sparrowhawks may be scouring the hedgerows, Marsh Harriers are seen on occasion in the area throughout the year, and Hen Harriers have been seen in winter. The Reserve attracts large Starling roosts in the autumn, and Peregrines soon cotton on to this ready source of food.

Up until now, at roughly the halfway point, the paths have been easy to follow and maintained by the RSPB with a covering of slate chippings, and are passable even after heavy rain. From this point on, however, the route will take you along public footpaths that are sometimes muddy, and across fields that can be marshy and churned up by cattle, which can be heavy going without appropriate footwear. Therefore, if you wish to keep clean feet, you can turn back at this point and retrace your steps to the car park; in the opposite direction, even the same footpath looks different! If you have suitable footwear and do not mind a bit of mud, the walk continues in a circular route back to the car park. The distance is not much more, and the onward section will take you closer to the birds lurking in the bushes and hidden channels amongst the reeds.

To take the circular walk, turn left at the bridge, and cross the stile to follow the track back across the fields. The track takes you through areas of reedbeds which tower over you as

Drake Teal

you walk, providing shelter and seed heads for Reed Buntings and Blue Tits. Continue round a slight bend past a ruined building on your right at the site of a former coal mine. The track straightens out again and passes through more marshland and another stand of tall reeds.

As you walk along here, check the marshy land on either side. In winter and early spring, you are likely to hear the soft 'trilling' of a group of Teal, and the whistling call of Wigeon, even if you cannot see the birds themselves on the pools of water. Coots and Moorhens can also be seen picking their way through the reed edges.

After about ¹/₄ mile/0.4 km, the path widens out slightly. To your right is a wooden five-barred gate, and to your left is a metal gate in stone gateposts giving onto a grassy field. Although it is not marked with a footpath sign, at this point the map shows a public footpath off to your left taking a straight line along the edge of the fields all the way back to the car park. However, these fields can be very boggy indeed and may be churned up even more by grazing cattle, so you may not wish to take this short cut.

To complete the full circular walk, continue straight ahead along the track which after a while gradually climbs up the slight rise in the land above the marshes. Continue up the track until you reach the main road, the B4419. Turn left here and walk along the road for approximately ¹/₂ mile/0.8 km. Take care

Swans in channel at Malltraeth

as traffic can sometimes drive very fast along here. Shortly having crossed a bridge over the disused railway and after a narrow lane forks off to your right, turn left down a track which descends rapidly before going under the old railway line. Continue under the bridge and past the historic Plas Berw on your left.

This is the ancestral home of the Holland family. The house dates from the early seventeenth century and has a courtyard garden which adjoins the ruins of an even older fifteenth-century dwelling. Around it is a deer park also dating from the fifteenth century, or possibly even earlier, with much of the original wall still standing.

Continue past the buildings, and when you reach the last one, turn right and climb the metal gate onto the footpath heading right, although it may not be clearly marked here, and may be muddy. The path takes a sharp left hand bend and continues until you reach a crossroads of tracks. Turn right here and continue straight ahead along this track for almost 1/2 mile/0.8 km until you reach a T-junction. Depending on where cattle or ponies are being grazed, the gates across these tracks may be closed to keep them in. If you do open any gates, please make sure you close them firmly after you. Turn left at the T-junction, and walk for about 1/4 mile/0.4 km with a stream on your right until you reach the car park.

What to look for …
… in spring: Lapwings and Curlews should be seen on the wet grassland.
… in summer: Meadow Pipits are likely on the grassy banks of the canalised Afon Cefni, and Skylarks are likely to be singing overhead. Sedge Warblers and Reed Warblers should be singing from the reedbeds and, if your luck is in, Grasshopper Warblers have been found here. Common Whitethroats may also put in

an appearance in the scrub bushes. Redshanks and Tufted Ducks both breed here and should be seen in the wet areas.

… in autumn: In August/September, Swallows roost here before their migration south, and from November, Starlings come here to roost, with attendant raptors hoping for an easy meal.

… in winter: Flocks of Pochard, Wigeon and Teal may be lurking in the marshy areas of the walk, Mute Swans are often seen on Afon Cefni or the parallel dyke, and Goosanders do also sometimes appear on the river at this time of year. This is a good time to look for Fieldfares and Redwings on the grassy areas.

… all year round: Reed Buntings can usually be seen in good numbers near the grassy bridge over Afon Cefni, as well as in the reedbeds along the track. Coots, Moorhens, Mallards, Shovellers and Gadwall are likely on Afon Cefni, while Grey Herons and Little Egret should be around in the smaller water channels or pools. Common Buzzards should be around, particularly along the back track to the car park, and Sparrowhawks may seen along the hedgerows.

Extreme rarities have been logged here at Malltraeth: Savi's Warbler in Spring/Summer, Night Heron in Summer, and Smew and Green-winged Teal have both been seen here in Winter – so keep your eyes open, who knows what you might find!

Where to eat:
The nearest place for food and drink is about five minutes' drive away. The licensed Gardener's Café at the Holland Arms Garden Centre (telephone 01248 421655) in Gaerwen serves hot and cold drinks, snacks and light meals. In your car, drive back along the track to the A5. Turn right heading towards Pentre Berw and Gaerwen. As you drive uphill after about $^1/_4$ mile/ 0.4 km, the Holland Arms Garden Centre is on your right.

Opening hours are 9 a.m. to 5.30 p.m., Monday to Saturday, 11 a.m. to 5 p.m. on Sunday.

The nearby town of Llangefni also holds a full range of amenities.

Other information:
- No facilities on site, nearest toilets at Holland Arms Garden Centre
- Wellingtons or waterproof walking boots recommended for the circular walk

What other sights are nearby:
- Newborough Forest and the island of Llanddwyn
- Town of Llangefni, and Anglesey art gallery, Oriel Môn

Cefni Reservoir and The Dingle, Llangefni

Site highlights:
- Easy walk offering a mixture of woodland, gently rolling countryside and views over open water
- Sculpture trail through The Dingle

Map and grid reference:
OS Map 114, Anglesey/Môn, SH459 765

Site directions:
From the A55 take the A5114 exit for Llangefni and follow the main road into the town centre. At a T-junction in the town centre, turn left onto the B5420. Turn right and follow the one-way system, following signs for the B5110 towards Benllech and the B5111 towards Amlwch. At a fork, turn left up a slight hill onto the B5111. After a left-hand bend, turn right at a brown sign for the Oriel Ynys Môn and golf course, and park in the car park here.

Headline description
This makes a very pleasant circular walk, particularly bird- and flower-rich in spring. Thanks to work on the Nature Reserve in recent years, much of the walking is on very well-maintained slate paths or boardwalks which lead you close to, and even in one place right on top of, the fast-flowing water of Afon Cefni! Meandering through the secluded woodland of The Dingle is particularly enjoyable in spring when it is full of bird song all around you and wild flowers at your feet. This makes a great contrast to the open space of the Cefni Reservoir with its population of wildfowl and gulls.

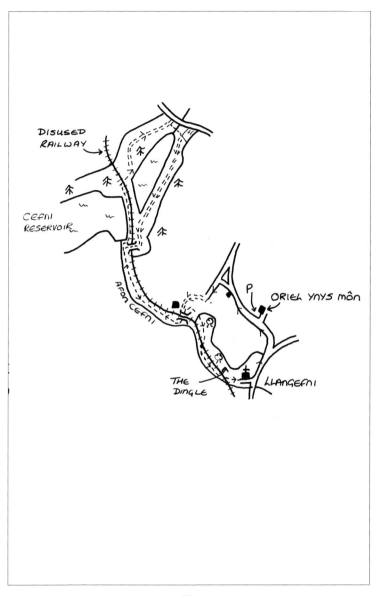

DISUSED
RAILWAY

CEFNI
RESERVOIR

Afon CEFNI

P

ORIEL YNYS môn

THE
DINGLE

LLANGEFNI

Length of walk:
Circular walk approximately 3 hours (5 miles/8 km)

Type of terrain:
Easy, mainly level walking on gravel and stone tracks.

Walk directions:
Check the car park before heading off on your walk. You are very likely to see Pied Wagtails strutting around the car park itself while the surrounding tall trees are a good place for the more common woodland birds such as Great Tit, Blue Tit, Chaffinch and Robin. Ravens can occur at any time on this walk, wheeling overhead; listen out for their distinctive 'kronk' call which can carry a long way. Other birds such as Woodpigeon, Magpies, Carrion Crows and Jackdaws are also likely here.

Leaving the car park at Oriel Ynys Môn, continue uphill along the main road for a short distance. Take care along this stretch; there is a pavement but the traffic tends to travel quite fast along here. After ¹/₄ mile/0.4 km, fork left onto a narrow lane called Pencoed. At the T-junction, turn left.

Check this stretch for hedgerow birds such as Dunnock and Wren. Fence posts and telegraph poles make good lookout posts for Buzzards, while Mistle Thrushes may be seen probing the grassy fields for food.

After a short distance you will reach a fork in the road. Continue straight ahead here, ignoring a track and cattle grid off to your right. Go through the footpath gate and follow the tarmac track as it descends down and right into the valley of Afon Cefni. Continue past the white cottage on your right until you reach the footpath in the valley and turn right. This is also a cycle path so it may become busier at peak times in the holiday season and at weekends. Go through the gate and under

The Dingle

the old railway bridge. Continue along the footpath with the disused railway on your right and Afon Cefni on your left.

This stretch of river used to be a good spot for Dipper, so keep your eyes peeled for this dapper brown bird with a white bib as it bobs up and down on small rocks in the river, in case one reappears. You are very likely to see a Grey Wagtail on this clear fast-flowing water too.

Ignore a footpath off to your left and continue along the slate track.

The area of scrubby bush and willows along the disused railway is a likely area in spring for migrants such as Common Whitethroats, Chiffchaffs, Willow Warblers and Blackcaps, so it is well worth checking this spot thoroughly. Keep an eye out at any time of year for Reed Buntings in the reeds to the left of the path, and you may also see Treecreepers working their way up the trunks of the trees here.

The path now crosses the river on a wooden bridge which then becomes a raised boardwalk. The path is cantilevered so it overhangs the river itself as the boardwalk clings to the side of the cliff, quite a feat of carpentry.

This is another good stretch to look for Dipper, while the reed beds on either side of the rusty railway tracks are a good place to look and listen for Reed and Sedge Warblers in spring. To be sure of your Reed Warbler, look out for its plain brown face lacking an obvious eye stripe and listen for its rather monotonous song which chugs along with very little variation in pitch. The Sedge Warbler on the other hand has a broad white eye stripe and has a more scratchy erratic song with much more variation in pitch.

Back on terra firma again, the now-concrete path crosses an area of floodplain, and the sign warns that the path itself is liable to flood!

This reedy area is another good spot for Sedge Warblers in spring, and may well conceal well-camouflaged Common Snipe too.

Continue through the wooden gate. You are now approaching Cefni Reservoir and because of the land levels here, you will experience the rather odd sensation of being at eye level with the water itself.

The area below the weir is covered in low scrub, ideal habitat for Cetti's Warblers, whose explosive calls may burst from well within the bush as the bird itself skulks out of sight. Check the stream below the weir for Grey Wagtails

Ignore the footpath heading off to the left, and continue walking towards the reservoir. As the slate path bends sharply to the right to zigzag up to the footbridge over the railway, leave the path here and climb up the grassy bank to the edge of the reservoir itself.

This is an excellent place to scan the open water. Coots are common here, and duck species should include Mallard and Tufted Duck all year, while winter visitors are likely to include Wigeon and Goldeneye. Canada and Greylag Geese can be found here all year, though the flocks may be larger in winter. This is a good place to look for gulls too: Black-headed and Common Gulls should be here all year, while Lesser Black-backed Gulls are possible from spring through to September. Look out for Great Crested Grebes displaying in spring and they should still be here in summer, while Little Grebes can be heard, if not seen, all year round.

Following the stone wall of the reservoir, continue to the right past the fence and walk across the causeway over the reservoir, following the track of the disused railway line. Walking across the middle of the water gives you a great opportunity to check for birds on both halves of this long, thin reservoir. On the far side of the water, the track continues into an area of pine forest. Follow the footpath off to the right into the trees. This area can be muddy but the path soon broadens out into a stony track.

Check the pine trees for forest birds such as Goldcrests and Coal Tits, looking for insects as they flit about amongst the pine needles. Blue Tits, Great Tits and Chaffinches are also likely here.

The path leads out of the trees to a viewing point over the reservoir and then continues as a broad track through the forest, as you keep the reservoir on your right.

A gully beside the track is often full of water. In early spring, this is a good place to look for frogspawn, though the frogs seem to prefer spawning in the shallower areas where there is greater risk of it drying out. Continue to keep a look out for Coal Tits and Goldcrests on the pines here, while Greenfinches and Bullfinches are also possible.

The track heads towards main road but just before you reach the road itself, a path leads off to your right with a little wooden bridge over the stream at the very head of the reservoir.

With the mixture of low willows and taller deciduous trees, this is a good place to look for Great Spotted Woodpecker all year round, while Willow Warblers and Chiffchaff are likely in the willows in spring and summer. You may often hear Ravens calling their rough 'kronking' call overhead, though the peace of the countryside is sometimes shattered by the roar of fighter jets overhead. Pilots from nearby RAF Valley practising their 'circuits and bumps' at nearby Mona Airfield will circle back to base over this area, flying sometimes alarmingly low and certainly making a lot of noise.

Follow the footpath to the car park.

It is worth spending a few minutes here to check the larches for Crossbills, while Coal Tits and Goldcrests are likely here as well as common woodland birds such as Robin, Blackbird, Chaffinch, Blue Tit and Great Tit.

Continue past the metal gate to walk along the broad track. The reservoir is now on your right and a path leads down to the water's edge where there used to be a bird hide. Unfortunately, this has burned down and not been replaced, but this still makes a good viewing spot over the reservoir. Continue along the track through more areas of willow.

In spring, this is a likely spot for Willow Warbler, Chiffchaff, Sedge Warbler, Blackcap and Garden Warbler. The view over the reservoir opens out again and it is worth having another scan across the water for any newcomers.

Cross the footbridge over the old disused railway and follow the zigzag path down to the water level. Continue back along the path, retracing your steps across the water meadows and along the raised boardwalk, with the disused railway on your left. Follow the footpath as it bends under the railway, but this time, instead of climbing up the hill past the white cottage, continue along the footpath as it enters an area of deciduous woodland, known as The Dingle.

The Dingle Local Nature Reserve received National Lottery funding in 2004 which together with other grant aid was put to great use here in improving the footpaths, building the boardwalks and involving the local community in creating a sculpture trail. The Dingle is also known as Nant y Pandy, or the Brook/Glen of the Fulling Mill, referring to a wool processing factory which used to operate further upstream. The steep gorge owes its formation to glacial meltwater gouging out the soft rock here, and this is one of Anglesey's few remaining areas of ancient woodland. Created as a Nature Reserve in 1995, the significance of this area has been recognised far longer; it has been known as The Dingle since the 1830s, though it took until 1971 for a tree preservation order to be put in place.

This is an excellent place to look for woodland birds such as Nuthatch, Treecreeper and Great Spotted Woodpecker which can be seen and heard making their way up, or down in the case of the Nuthatch, the trees here. You may be lucky enough to see a Jay here too as well as the regular woodland birds such as Robin, Blackbird, Dunnock, Chaffinch, Blue Tit and Great Tit. In early summer you should also be able to see, or at least hear, Chiffchaff, Willow Warbler and Blackcap in the bushes. In spring, the ground becomes a blue and white carpet as Bluebells and Wood Anemones burst into flower.

The slate paths and wooden boardwalks meander their way through this attractive hidden stretch of woodland and rocky stream and all lead to the same place. However, cyclists must keep to the slate paths so you may find it quieter to walk along the boardwalks at busy times. You are more likely to catch sight of a Grey Wagtail picking its way along the edge of the river too.

Whichever route you prefer, you should pass where the river broadens out into a small lake and arrive at a crossroads of paths. Follow the fingerpost to the church, keeping the river on your right. You will shortly pass St Cyngar's Well. The footpath emerges from The Dingle with St Cyngar's church on your left. Walk across the car park to the main road. Turn left by the funeral directors' premises and walk along the road leading out of Llangefni. After a short distance, you will reach where the B5111 forks off to the left. Follow this road uphill, and you will very quickly reach the car park of the Oriel Ynys Môn on your right.

What to look for …
… in spring/summer: Look out for the arrival of spring migrants particularly in the areas of willow, where you may encounter Willow Warblers, Chiffchaffs, Common Whitethroats,

Male Reed Bunting

Blackcaps, Garden Warblers. In the reedy areas, listen out for Sedge and Reed Warblers calling, while Cetti's Warbler song may burst out of the scrubby bushes below the weir. Lesser

Black-backed Gulls may start appearing out on the open water of the reservoir at this time of year, as well as Great Crested Grebes: look out for them performing their stunning mating dance. Swifts, Swallows, Sand and House Martins are likely to be hawking over the water for insects as spring progresses into summer. Ospreys have been seen on their northerly migration but you would be very lucky to see one!

… in autumn: Wildfowl numbers out on the reservoir start to build up with the arrival of Pochard, Gadwall, Shoveler, Teal, Goldeneye and Wigeon; the shallow east end is the best area. There have also been occasional records of Garganey here in August and September. Check the flocks of Teal carefully, as Garganey will sometimes associate with them.

… in winter: Check the fields at the start of your walk for Fieldfares and Redwings looking for food amongst the grass. You should still be able to see the autumn duck arrivals at this time of year, and bird numbers on the reservoir will also be boosted by gull species such as Black-headed and Common Gulls. Check the flocks carefully for scarcer species. Mediterranean Gulls have occurred here on a number of occasions and a Glaucous Gull on rare occasions. If you are very lucky, you may flush a Woodcock from the damp wooded area on the far side of the reservoir, while similarly, Common Snipe may lurk in the reeds and rough grasses of the water meadows beside the disused railway. A small flock of Whooper Swans winters on fields north of the reservoir and occasionally visits the water. Early mornings can be the best time to see them. Peregrine Falcons hunt the area but tend to move through very quickly, so you will have to be alert to see one.

… all year round: Resident hedgerow birds such as Dunnock, Wren, Robin, Blackbird, Song and Mistle Thrushes should put in an appearance along the peaceful lanes at the start of your walk. You are likely to see Reed Buntings in the reedbeds beside the disused railway line at any time of year. You should see some species of wildfowl at any time of year out on the reservoir, such as Mallard, Tufted Duck, Greylag and Canada Geese, Mute Swan, while Little Grebe, Moorhen and Coot will also be there. In the woodland areas, you should be able to find Goldcrests, as well as Coal, Great, Blue and Long-tailed Tits at any time of year, while Great Spotted Woodpeckers, Nuthatches, and Jays make themselves heard if not always seen. Sharp eyes may pick out a Treecreeper working its way up the treetrunk. Buzzards and Ravens are easy to see and you may also see the occasional Kestrel or Sparrowhawk. If you are lucky, you may also encounter Crossbills and Lesser Redpolls in any larch trees; around the car park is a particularly good spot.

Where to eat:
Within the same building as the Oriel Ynys Môn is the popular licensed café Blas Mwy, which is open seven days a week from 10.30 a.m. to 5 p.m. It offers hot and cold drinks, homemade snacks, cakes and light meals.

Other information:
- Free parking at Oriel Ynys Môn
- Toilets and gift shop in the art gallery building

What other sights are nearby:
- Malltraeth RSPB Reserve
- The historic suspension bridge and town of Menai Bridge
- Church Island and views of the Menai Strait

Cemlyn Bay

Site highlights:
- Close views of one of Britain's largest tern colonies in breeding season
- High occurrence of rare and unusual species
- Variety of habitat including saltwater lagoon, shoreline, pasture and scrubland
- Easy walking in stunning coastal scenery

Map and grid reference:
OS Map 114 (Anglesey/Môn), SH 329 936

Site directions:
Leave the A55 at the Valley exit. Take the A5 north towards Valley, and at the traffic lights, turn right, heading north on the A5025 heading towards Cemaes. Turn left onto a narrow minor road at Caerdegog Uchaf, where the A road bends to the right (grid reference SH 343 914) and immediately left again with the disused windmill to your right. Follow this narrow lane and ignore the next turning to the left signposted Llanfairynghornwy. Continue on this twisty lane for about 2 miles/3.2 km. Turn left, and after ½ mile/0.8 km, bear right, keeping the lagoon on your right. Continue along this lane over the bridge, and continue alongside the high brick wall to the large car park at the end.

Note: at extreme tides, the sea may rise to cover part of the car park, so it is advisable to park away from the water's edge.

An alternative car park can be found at the other end of the shingle ridge (grid ref SH 337 932). To reach this, follow the

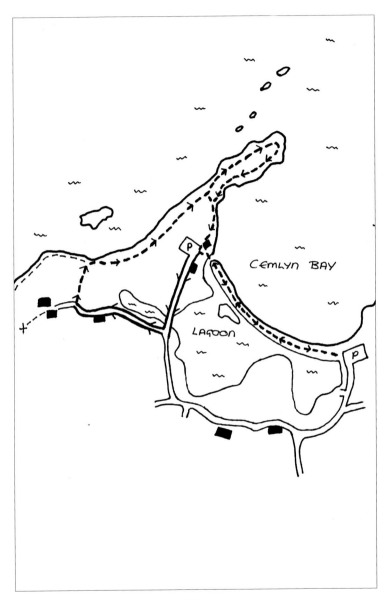

CEMLYN BAY

LAGOON

same route as above. After following the twisty lane for 2 miles/3.2 km, do not turn left but continue round to the right and take the left fork to the car park at the next junction.

Headline description
'Expect the unexpected' must be the watchword for this birding mecca on the Welsh mainland. Only the island of Bardsey Llŷn can beat Cemlyn for attracting good birds and rarities throughout the year. The list of stunning unusual and rare birds to pop up here over the years is long and illustrious, and includes such far-flung travellers as American Golden Plover, Lesser Yellowlegs, Black-winged Stilts, Cayenne Tern, Sooty Tern, Bridled Tern, Black-headed Bunting, Woodchat Shrike and Blue-winged Teal, to name but some. Visit here in the breeding season, and even if there are no rarities about, you will still enjoy stunning close-up views of the amazing tern colony on the lagoon. The variety of habitat, including saltwater lagoon, rough pasture, rocky shoreline and scrubby bush ensures a range of waders, wildfowl, shorebirds and passerines are there for you to discover at any time of year. Add the possibility of seeing seals and dolphins from this stunning coastline, and you can appreciate the appeal of this wonderful place and want to return here again and again.

Length of walk:
Approximately 2 hours (2 miles/3.2 km)

Type of terrain:
Shingle beach. Metalled lane and grassy paths on the headland, muddy in places; walking further recommended.

Walk directions:
Firstly, if the tide permits, it is well worth walking out onto the shingle ridge to view the bay and island on the lagoon.

From the car park, walk over the flat rocks beside the high stone wall towards the sea. Cross the outlet stream by the concrete causeway and make your way out onto the shingle ridge. Note: at high

The beach at Cemlyn

tide, these rocks are covered and the stream flows surprisingly fast over the causeway. You can still wade across but the water may be deeper and colder than you expect. I speak from experience!

This shingle ridge, or esgair, has been formed by the action of the waves and wind depositing rocks and shingle across the bay to create a lagoon trapped behind it. This lagoon is fed by a freshwater stream, with an input of saltwater at high tides only. The protected brackish water that results is a haven for waders and wildfowl, and the site is managed as a nature reserve by the North Wales Wildlife Trust on lease from the National Trust, which owns much of this coastline. This spot regularly attracts unusual species: the regulars such as Red-breasted Mergansers, Shelducks, Redshanks, Oystercatchers and Ringed Plovers have in the past been joined by more scarce species such as Garganey, Red-necked Phalarope, American Golden Plover, Terek Sandpiper, and Blue-winged Teal.

The island on the lagoon holds one of Britain's largest tern colonies during the spring breeding season. Excellent views can be had of the Sandwich, Common and Arctic Terns from the shingle ridge, though people are asked to keep to a restricted viewing area during certain months so as to minimise any disruption to the birds. The close views of these birds, either sitting on eggs or commuting continuously to and fro with fish, as well as the noise and smell from this bustling colony, will make a lasting impression upon you. Again, in addition to the more common species, this colony has over the years attracted such unusual visitors as Cayenne, Sooty, Bridled, Caspian and Whiskered Terns.

You cannot fail to notice Wylfa nuclear power station in the distance. It was the last and largest of its type to be built, and has been supplying electricity since 1971. It is scheduled to close down in 2010, at which point the fuel will be gradually removed and sent to Sellafield to be treated.

Retrace your steps back to the car park, and walk back down the lane, with the brick wall to your left until you reach the bridge.

Where you cross the bridge, take the time to scan back across the lagoon to view the other side of the tern island. It is also worth studying the narrow body of water on your right for any birds that may be quietly skulking in the edge of the reeds.

Turn right and walk along the farm lane beside the lake, checking the bushes, fields and water for birds. After a right-hand bend, just before you reach the farm, go through a field gate on your right and walk slightly uphill towards the coast, keeping to the left hand edge of the field.

These marshy fields can be rather muddy underfoot, but can also hold birds such as Yellow Wagtails, Meadow Pipits, Linnets, and have even provided a temporary resting spot for Black-winged Stilts, Pectoral Sandpiper, Lesser Yellowlegs, Tawny Pipits and Lapland Buntings. The marsh flowers,

Common Tern

including Flag Iris, add a bold note of colour here in summer.

At the top of the field where you reach the cliff edge, you join the Anglesey Coastal Path. For this walk, turn right and continue through a series of kissing gates along the field edges, with the rocky shore on your left.

Check the shore for any birds down amongst the rocks, including Oystercatchers, Turnstones, Cormorants and gulls. If you are lucky, you may spot Grey Seals either resting full length on the small island just offshore or bobbing about in the water, casting a curious eye over any walkers nearby. Dolphins have also been seen offshore, more frequently Bottlenosed Dolphins, but pods of Risso's Dolphins have also been recorded.

A wooden bench looking out to sea provides a convenient resting place for scanning the sea and shore. From here, you can walk around the grassy headland for a view of the bay. Alternatively, take the footpath to your right which leads directly back to the car park.

You will pass a memorial commemorating the 150th anniversary of the first lifeboat commissioned on Anglesey (1828-1978). This service was founded by the Reverend James Williams and his wife Frances, after they witnessed the death of 145 people when the Irish Packetboat, The 'Alert', ran aground on West Mouse island in 1823.

Right up until the minute you drive off in your car, it is worth checking the shoreline and the bushes and fields around the car park. The scrubby bushes have in the past provided cover for Common Rosefinch, Woodchat Shrike and Melodious Warbler, so you can almost expect the unexpected here.

What to look for …
… in late spring/summer: You cannot miss the tern colony on the island in the lagoon. Look out for Common, Sandwich and Arctic Terns, while occasionally Roseate Terns still visit this site. Rare terns have also frequented the lagoon, including Cayenne, Sooty, Bridled, Caspian and Whiskered Terns. The island also attracts nesting Black-headed Gulls.
… in summer: As you walk across the fields, you should see and hear Skylarks singing on the wing, while Meadow Pipits and Linnets rise up at your feet. Check the damp field beside the narrow lane towards the farm for Yellow Wagtail.
… in autumn: Looking out to sea, you may catch sight of Fulmars, Manx Shearwaters and Gannets flying past. Along the shoreline, keep an eye open for Purple Sandpipers, Dunlins, Whimbrels, Common Sandpipers and Turnstones. Other waders such as Golden Plovers, Grey Plovers, Lapwings and Knots are also likely here. Snow Buntings may be seen, and Wheatears on passage too. And of course, this is Cemlyn, so scarce and rare migrants may also turn up.
… in winter: Red-breasted Mergansers, some Teal and Wigeon should be seen on the lagoon, and other duck such as Goldeneye and Gadwall may occur.

… all year round: At any time of year you should see Shelducks on the lagoon and Grey Herons fishing on its edges. Along the shoreline, look out for Redshanks, Oystercatchers, Cormorants and gulls, and look across to the little islands just offshore, and you're likely to see Grey Seals, either basking on the island or bobbing in the water here. Meadow Pipits and Stonechats should be easy to see on the grassland and fenceposts. Looking upwards, you should see Buzzards over the farmland, while Ravens and Choughs are more likely to be enjoying the thermals along the coastline.

Where to eat:
'The Jam Factory' at the nearby hamlet of Nanner (grid Ref SH 335 920) makes jam and honey on the premises for sale, and also has a Coffee and Tea Shop offering hot and cold drinks, snacks and homemade cakes. Telephone: 01407 711 588.

Other information:
- Free car park
- No public toilets on site, the nearest are in Cemaes. Toilets at The Jam Factory for customers only
- Causeway to shingle beach covered at high tide, and car park may be flooded by exceptional tides
- The North Wales Wildlife Trusts viewing instructions to be followed to avoid disturbance during breeding season

What other sights are nearby:
- Anglesey Coastal Path in both directions
- National Trust coastline at Carmel Head is a good birding area
- Point Lynas with its lighthouse is an excellent spot for sea-watching
- Wylfa Nuclear Power Station, visitor centre is open 10 a.m. to 4 p.m. daily, free entrance, café on-site

Point Lynas (*Trwyn Eilian*)

Site highlights:
- An excellent spot for sea-watching with sensational numbers of birds passing in the right conditions
- Attractive coastal scenery at one of the best places in northern Wales to see Harbour Porpoises

Map and grid reference:
OS Map 114 (Anglesey/Môn), SH 474 928

Site directions:
Take the A5025 out of Amlwch, heading south. After about a mile/1.6 km, you reach a crossroads of two minor roads with the A road. Take the lane to the left signposted for Llaneilian. Follow on this lane for about 2 miles/3.2 km towards Llaneilian, ignoring other minor roads to your right and left. Just after passing a church with a spire on your left, take a sharp bend left into Llaneilian. As the road starts to go downhill, leave your car in a free public car park on the right-hand side and walk to Point Lynas from here (approximately one mile/1.6 km). Alternatively you can drive out some distance onto the point itself to a parking area (fee sometimes payable).

Headline description
This has to be one of the best places in northern Wales to sit and watch large numbers of seabirds and passage migrants flying past you. Given the right season and weather conditions (a good north-westerly wind), birds have been seen passing in tens of thousands. Even out of peak birding season, it is still possible to get good views of seabirds flying past, diving for fish or mobbing one another. And to make any outing complete, this is

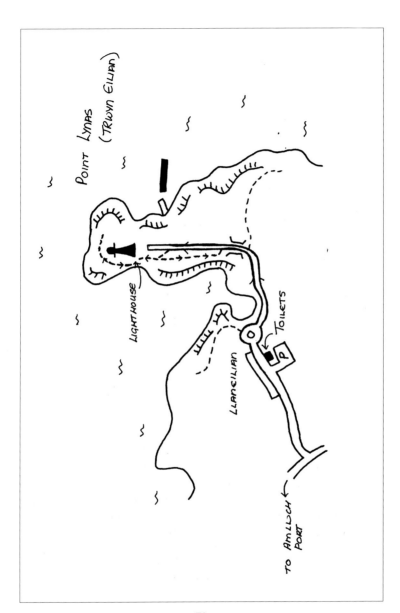

Point Lynas
(Trwyn Eilian)

LIGHTHOUSE

LLANEILIAN

Toilets
P

TO AMLWCH
PORT

probably the best site in northern Wales to see Harbour Porpoises just offshore. The wind will nearly always blow here on this exposed point, but you will be rewarded with stunning views up and down the coastline.

Length of walk:
Approximately 1¹/₂ hours (2 miles/3.2 km from public car park)

Type of terrain:
Metalled lane and grassy paths on the headland

Walk directions:
Leaving the car park, continue along the lane downhill, passing the public toilets. At the bottom of the hill is a mini-roundabout.

You can access the narrow bay of Porth Eilian here, and it is worth taking time to scan the water and cliffs here for seabirds, including Cormorants, Gulls and even Black Guillemots. Choughs can usually be seen and heard around here, as they ride the air currents over the cliffs.

Bear right at the roundabout, keeping the bay on your left, and continue along the lane past the cattle grid. Follow the track towards the lighthouse at the end.

As you walk, check the bushes along the road for passage migrants which may have dropped down for shelter here, particularly after an easterly wind has been blowing. Birds seen here have included Wheatears, Snow Buntings, Black Redstarts, Lapland Buntings and even Red-breasted Flycatcher, so in season, keep your eyes peeled for a rarity.

As you approach the lighthouse and the 'No Access' sign on the road, take the footpath marked to the left of the buildings

Bay at Point Lynas

and follow this round out onto the headland in front of the lighthouse. The buildings are now privately owned, and walkers are encouraged by low wooden barriers not to stray from the path.

Take your time here to scan the sea with your telescope for birds such as Auks, Gannets, Kittiwakes, Gulls, Terns, Cormorants, Shearwaters and even Skuas. When conditions are right, you can enjoy a steady stream of seabirds passing below you in their thousands, many close enough to enjoy reasonable views even just with binoculars. Harbour Porpoises can also be seen quite frequently off the point, providing the sea is not too rough to give good visibility.

Retrace your steps to the car park, birding as you go.

What to look for ...
... in spring: Looking out to sea, you should pick up Manx

Shearwaters, Sandwich Terns and Gannets flying past the headland. On land, look out for Wheatears pausing on their spring migration north.

... in summer: You are still likely to see Manx Shearwaters, Sandwich Terns and Gannets flying past the headland.

... in autumn: Perhaps the best time to visit for sea-watching. Look out for seabirds on migration, as anything can and does occur here in onshore winds! Apart from the regular Manx Shearwaters, from the headland in the right conditions you may be lucky enough (with a telescope!) to see rarities such as Balearic Shearwaters, Storm Petrel and Leach's Petrel. Common Scoter may be on the water, while skua species including Arctic, Great and even on occasion Pomarine Skua may be seen. Look out for divers and grebes on the water, as well as wildfowl and waders migrating past the headland. On land, you may see Wheatear this time migrating south, while other rarer birds such

Cliffs at Point Lynas

Shag

as Black Redstarts, Snow Bunting and Lapland Bunting may turn up in more sheltered spots.

... in winter: Along the shoreline, look out for Turnstones and Purple Sandpipers. You may be lucky enough to see a Black Redstart in more sheltered areas.

... all year round: Check the bay for Cormorants and Shags, gulls and Black Guillemots. Rock Pipits may be flitting around the rocks themselves, while overhead you may well see Choughs and Ravens enjoying the air currents. Look out for Peregrines flashing through on the hunt for prey, and Kestrels hovering overhead having spotted a potential meal. Along the lane you should see Stonechats, usually perched on top of a convenient bush or post, or Linnets often gathering on the ground.

Lighthouse at Point Lynas

Where to eat:
In previous years a tea bar at Porth Eilian offered hot and cold drinks and sweets. However, at time of going to print, the tea bar was no longer there. A good alternative, less than ten minutes' drive away, is The Sail Loft Café, at the nearby Heritage Centre at Amlwch Port, open from Easter until September. Opening hours are 10 a.m. to 2 p.m. Easter to beginning of May, 10 a.m. to 5 p.m. beginning of May to end of September. Leave Llaneilian along the same lane on which you arrived, but after just over a mile/1.6 km turn right towards Amlwch. You will start to enter the residential outskirts of Amlwch, and about 1 mile/1.6 km past the junction, turn right down a narrow lane where a brown sign indicates the Heritage

Centre at Amlwch Port. Continue to the end of the lane and park in the free car park here. Walk back to the Heritage Centre and The Sail Loft Café, which serves hot and cold drinks, snacks and homemade cakes. The café contains a display on the history of the area and the development of the port itself which is worth exploring before you leave. You can also walk out onto the headland of Llam Carw from where you can look back along the coastline to Point Lynas.

Other information:
- Free car park and public toilets in Llaneilian
- Further parking out on the Point, fee sometimes payable
- Telescope advisable for best birding views on the Point

What other sights are nearby:
- Cemlyn Bay coastline and lagoon
- Carmel Head for coastal walking
- Anglesey Coastal Path in both directions

Penmon

Site highlights:
- An enjoyable circular walk leading to the picturesque headland of Penmon, with its dramatic lighthouse and stunning views of Puffin Island (*Ynys Seiriol*) and Eryri/Snowdonia
- An excellent spot for watching seabirds passing quite close to land
- A mixture of hedgerows and heathland providing suitable places to look for passing migrants
- Attractive historic ruins of Penmon Priory and Dovecote

Map and grid reference:
OS Map 114 (Anglesey/Môn), SH 630 807

Site directions:
Take the A55 North Wales Expressway across the Britannia Bridge over the Menai Strait on the Isle of Anglesey. Take the first exit, a few hundred yards immediately after the bridge. At the bottom of the slip road, turn right onto the A5 towards Menai Bridge. After about 1¼ miles/2 km, you will reach a roundabout. Take the right-hand exit, continuing on the A5. After ¼ mile/0.4 km, you reach a second roundabout. Turn left onto the A545 to Beaumaris. Follow this road as it leads through the busy village of Menai Bridge and then continues along the attractive Anglesey coast to Beaumaris, about 4 miles/6.4 km from Menai Bridge. Drive straight through Beaumaris and continue on this road, passing Beaumaris Castle on your left, as the road becomes the B5109 to Llangoed. Approximately 2½ miles/4 km after passing the castle, you reach a crossroads of two minor roads. Take the turning on the right, signposted to

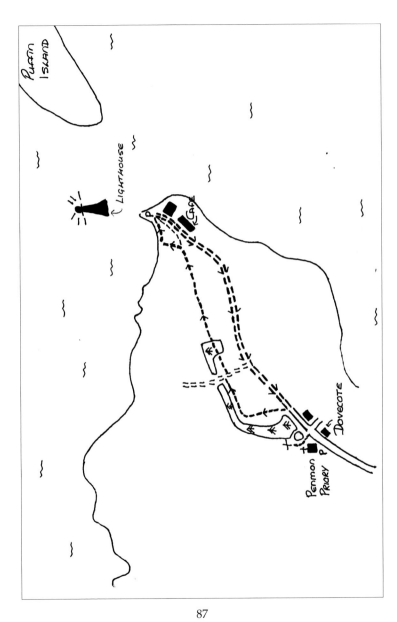

PUFFIN ISLAND

LIGHTHOUSE

CAGE

DOVECOTE

Penmon Priory

Penmon. Follow this minor road, taking care at some of the very sharp bends and narrow stretches, for about 3 miles/4.8 km, until you reach the ruins of Penmon Priory. To follow the walk, park here and follow the walking directions to Penmon. Alternatively, if you do not wish to walk at all, you can drive right out to the Point itself. In either case, a small fee is payable in season.

Headline description
This is an excellent walk which can be enjoyed at any time of year, though it may be rather blowy in winter. You will follow paths across a mixture of farmland and heathland out to the coast itself, and be rewarded with fine views of the Anglesey coastline and Puffin Island (*Ynys Seiriol*), as well as the north coast of the mainland and the mountains of Eryri/Snowdonia. The bushes lining the fields and dotted about the heathland provide shelter for smaller resident birds and migrants in spring and autumn, while time spent sea-watching at the point itself is likely to give you excellent views of seabirds and mammals in this beautiful setting. Add a sprinkling of culture in the form of Penmon Priory ruins, and a friendly café to restore you at the furthest point on your walk, and what more could you ask!

Length of walk:
Approximately $1^1/_2$ hours (2 miles/3.2 km)

Type of terrain:
Grassy footpaths and metalled lane on the headland. Some areas can be muddy after rain.

Walk directions:
If you have parked beside Penmon Priory, it is worth taking a look at the historic buildings before setting off on your walk.

There is said to have been a monastery here since the sixth

Aerial view of Penmon and Puffin Island

century, founded by St Seiriol, but most evidence was destroyed by Viking raids. In the twelfth century, the priory church was rebuilt, and is still in use today. In the thirteenth century, Penmon became a more substantial Augustinian priory, but it was dissolved in 1538. The land and buildings were acquired by the Bulkeley family from Beaumaris, who also built the square dovecote around 1600 to house around a thousand doves in cubby holes in the walls.

Opposite the dovecote, take the footpath signposted St Seiriol's Well, passing the monks' fishpond on your right.

You can sometimes see Brown Trout in this pool, and a family party of Moorhens is usually in residence, while dragonflies skim the water in summer. Check the bushes overhanging the water for Willow Warblers, members of the tit family, House Sparrows and finches, while in summer Swallows may swoop over the water to snatch a drink or scoop up hovering insects. Continuing on to the site of St Seiriol's Well, the original well is supposed to date from the sixth century, although the upper building around it was built in the eighteenth century.

Retrace your steps back to the dovecote and turn left to walk uphill up the lane. Passing a cottage to your right, you reach a field entrance to your left where you should climb over the ladder stile into the field. Continue forwards across the field heading for a wall and a stand of pine trees on the far side. When you reach the trees, bear right and follow along beside the bushes at the edge of the field. This section can sometimes be a little soggy underfoot.

As you walk along, check all the bushes and trees carefully for sheltering birds such as Chaffinches, Greenfinches, Goldfinches, Bullfinches, Willow Warblers, Chiffchaffs, Common Whitethroats and Goldcrests. Look up and you may see a raptor overhead: Buzzards are sometimes seen circling, or if you are lucky, a Peregrine may chase through.

At the end of the field, you reach a small lane. Turn right and then immediately left at the footpath signs, to follow another path along the edge of the next field, again checking the bushes for birds as you go. Climb the ladder stile and continue along the footpath through a little copse of small trees and scrubby bush. This section can be rather muddy, so do take care. You emerge from this copse into a more open area of heathland and bracken with willows, hawthorn, rowan, sloes and blackberry bushes dotted about.

Again this is a good area to see warblers such as Chiffchaffs and Willow Warblers, so it is worth checking all the bushes carefully, stopping to both look and listen

Black Guillemot

As you round a bend, you get your first view of Puffin Island and the lighthouse of Penmon, and hear the mournful clang of its bell. Follow the steps downhill, and at the brow of the small hill, the path splits, with the right hand path heading straight towards the Coastguards' Cottages. Take the left-hand path which winds its way down to the shoreline before heading towards the cottages on the Point.

As you walk along, check the shoreline for Oystercatchers, Turnstones, and other shore waders. At the Point itself, it is worth taking the time to sit and do a spot of sea-watching.

Looking across to Puffin Island, you are likely to see roosts of Cormorants, Guillemots and Razorbills on the island or on the water, and a small number of Puffins, though these are easier to see with a telescope. In summer, keep an eye out for other seabirds such as Sandwich Terns and Gannets passing through between their breeding colonies and fishing sites, as well as various gulls, and duck such as Common Scoter and Eider. You may be lucky enough to see Grey Seals keeping a curious eye on the human activity, and Harbour Porpoise and Dolphin have also been seen here.

One of the Pilot's Cottages here has been converted into a café, providing a welcome pit-stop before the walk back.

To return to your car, follow the narrow lane for about a mile back to the Priory, ignoring any side turnings. It is worth taking the time to check the bushes on either side of the road for a last chance to see more passerines.

What to look for …
… in summer: If you look with binoculars out from the Point towards Puffin Island you should see seabirds such as Fulmars, Kittiwakes, Guillemots, Razorbills, Gannets and Sandwich Terns flying past, and if you are lucky maybe a Puffin too. Of course, a telescope will give you much better views of these sometimes distant birds. The bushes beside the path and dotted over the heathland are the best place to look for Common and Lesser Whitethroats, Blackcaps, Chiffchaffs, Willow Warblers and Sedge Warblers, though you may see warblers in the bushes around the fishpond too.
… in winter: Looking off the Point, you may see Red-throated Divers, Great Crested Grebes and Red-breasted Mergansers on the water
… all year round: Check the large rocks on the shoreline for Cormorants and Shags gathering, while Oystercatchers and Rock Pipits may be busy on the smaller stones by the water's edge. Stonechats and Meadow Pipits may sit up on the heathland bushes, and don't forget to look upwards: Peregrines, Buzzards, Ravens and even Choughs may be flying overhead.

Where to eat:
The Pilot House Café, in a converted lighthouse pilot's cottage

Penmon and lighthouse

at Penmon, offers hot and cold drinks and snacks, ices and homemade cakes. The café is open daily from 9 a.m. – 6 p.m. in summer, and during daylight hours at the weekends only in winter. You may wish to call to check opening hours on 07776 006804.

Other information:
- Parking available at Penmon Priory and at the far end of Penmon.
- Parking fee payable in season for either parking site.
- No public toilets; toilets at café for customers only
- Use of a telescope will give much better views of passing seabirds from Penmon

On your drive to or from Penmon, you may wish to stop at Penrhyn Point (*Trwyn y Penrhyn*, grid reference SH 629 798) for a spot of extra birding. Where the lane bends sharply beside a

Dovecote at Penmon Priory

muddy and sandy bay, a short stretch of the old road makes a good place to park if you wish to take a look for any birds around. The rocks on the shore that are exposed at low tide make a good resting place for gulls, terns and cormorants, and if you check the rocky beach carefully, you are likely to see Oystercatchers, Turnstones and maybe Rock Pipits pottering about amongst the stones. If you cross over the road, take a look at the small pool and the surrounding field here where you may see Canada and Greylag Geese, Grey Herons, Redshanks, Curlews and other waders. This little corner has also provided a brief stopover for such rarities as Red-backed Shrike.

What other sights are nearby:
- Historic town and castle in Beaumaris
- Menai Bridge and Church Island
- University town of Bangor
- Anglesey Coastal Path

Church Island and Menai Bridge

Site highlights:
- Attractive spot on the Menai Strait at water level giving spectacular views of the Menai Suspension Bridge and Britannia Bridge
- Access to the Anglesey Coastal Path
- Close views of waders on the mudflats exposed at low tide

Map and grid reference:
OS Map 114 (Anglesey/Môn), SH 554 718

Site directions:
Take the A5 onto Anglesey over the Menai Suspension Bridge. Go straight on at the roundabout, following the A5. Continue past the supermarket and, immediately after the Chinese restaurant on your left, turn left into the car park. If you reach the next roundabout, you have gone too far and need to retrace your steps.

Headline description
This is an easy, short walk along the Menai Strait which allows you to appreciate the narrowness of the channel and the speed of the water-flow through it. Passing under the Menai Suspension Bridge gives you a view from an unusual angle of this spectacular bridge. With birds collecting on the rocky islets and exploring the exposed mudflats around Church Island, you can often get good close-up views of waders and wildfowl.

Length of walk:
Approximately 1¹/₂ hours (1¹/₂ miles/2.4 km)

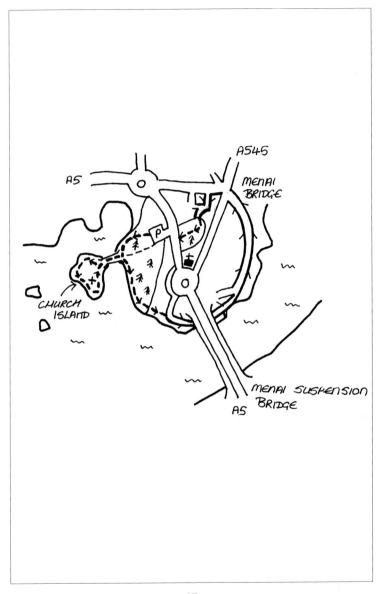

Type of terrain:
Easy walking, tarmac path and quiet lanes

Walk directions:
From the car park, take the footpath beside the information board and follow this downhill through the woodlands.

This rocky headland used to be common land, and signs of ancient civilisations here have been discovered as relics of Early Bronze Age cremation burials, Bronze Age axes and Roman coins have all been found here. The land was planted up as woodland by the Marquis of Anglesey who acquired it in 1814. It was then passed to the council in 1949, and opened to public in 1951 as part of the Festival of Britain.

At the bottom of the steps, turn left and follow the footpath downhill through the woods.

Nuthatch

As you walk through the woodland, keep your eyes and ears open for Great Spotted Woodpeckers, Treecreepers, Jays and other woodland birds. This is also one place on Anglesey where you are likely to find a Nuthatch.

At the bottom of the hill, join the tarmac track and turn right, crossing the causeway out onto the island of St Tysilio's Church. Walk around the footpath skirting the bottom of the island and enjoy the views of the Strait, the bridges and the birds.

At low tide, large areas of mud may be exposed and you are likely to see waders and wildfowl here. Little Egrets, Grey Heron, Cormorants and, in winter, Shags, are all likely to be seen on the rocky islets, while Oystercatchers, Curlews, Redshanks and gulls may be exploring the mudbanks. In summer, you may see Common Terns feeding over the Strait, and in winter, Red-breasted Mergansers can often be seen on the water.

At the far end of the island, a conveniently-placed seat allows you to sit and contemplate the Britannia Bridge, carrying both road and rail traffic to and from the island and mainland. You can also appreciate the racing, sometimes treacherous, tide through this particularly narrow stretch of the Strait, and imagine life in the solitary house situated on an island in the middle of this fast-flowing waterway. The path loops round the island passing the tiny church dedicated to St Tysilio, in the middle of its tranquil churchyard of slate headstones.

This church was built in the fifteenth century, though it is probably based on the foundations of a much older building. Legend has it that Tysilio was the son of a powerful ruler of Powys, Brochfael Ysgythrog, in the sixth century. Brochfael wanted his son to follow in his warring footsteps, but Tysilio wanted to pursue a religious life and fled here to escape his father, and founded his church.

Crossing the causeway back to the mainland, you can return direct to the car park up the tarmac track, if time is very limited. Alternatively, for a longer circular walk, turn right and follow the tarmac path round the base of the headland.

This stretch is known as Belgian Promenade, after the refugees who found safety and shelter here in Menai Bridge in 1914, and who built this promenade in 1916 for the community, as a way to express their thanks. Unfortunately the original structure had to be repaired after being damaged by flooding in the 1960s.

As you continue round the bend, you have impressive close up views of the Menai Suspension Bridge. Follow the path uphill past the steps down onto the foreshore. At the top of the path, turn right onto the narrow road and turn right again after a short distance at the Anglesey Coastal Path sign. The path leads you through a little beech clearing with standing stones of the Gorsedd Circle, commemorating the National Eisteddfod at Menai Bridge.

Although only a small area, the trees can be full of birdsong and you may have good close-up views of woodland birds such as Coal Tits and Goldcrests.

The path rejoins the lane and passes under the Menai Suspension Bridge itself. Continue along this narrow lane, past houses enjoying magnificent views of the Strait and the Bridge.

The swirling waters of the Strait have proven a barrier to invaders from Roman times onwards. A ferry has always existed here for centuries, and despite the difficult waters, a large number of ships used the Strait as the route to reach

Saint Tysilio's Church

Conwy. The challenge was to build a bridge carrying the main London to Holyhead highway across this narrow strip, whilst still allowing sailing vessels to pass underneath. Thomas Telford was given this task, which he achieved by building the world's longest suspension bridge at that time, some 1500 feet/457 m long with its carriageway 100 feet/30 m above the waters below.

Continue along this road past the bowling green, public toilets and launching slip at Prince's Pier. Continue along Water Street past the marina and Liverpool Arms pub, until you reach the junction with main road at Uxbridge Square in the middle of the village of Menai Bridge. If you turn right here, you will pass three cafés.

To return to your car from this point, cross over the road into Dale Street and turn left up the one-way road immediately before the former chapel, now turned greengrocer. Opposite is the film set for the Welsh TV soap opera 'Rownd a Rownd'. After a short distance at the end of this one-way road, cross over the road and take the footpath opposite you up through the woods between the library building and a block of apartments.

Again, although this is only a small patch of woodland, it can hold a surprising number of birds including Coal Tits, Long-tailed Tits, and even Jays.

After a short distance, you emerge onto the main road opposite the Chinese restaurant and the car park from where you started your walk.

What to look for …
… in summer: Common Terns feeding in the Menai Strait.
… in winter: Little Egrets, Cormorants, Grey Herons, Greylag Goose, Shelduck, Oystercatchers on the water's edge, exposed mudflats and islets; Nuthatches, Treecreepers, Jays, Great Spotted Woodpeckers, Coal Tits, Sparrowhawks in the woodland areas; Buzzards circling overhead; Peregrine Falcons on Britannia Bridge.
… all year round: Little Egrets, Cormorants, Grey Herons, Greylag Goose, Shelduck, Oystercatchers on the water's edge, exposed mudflats and islets; Nuthatches, Treecreepers, Jays, Great Spotted Woodpeckers, Coal Tits, Sparrowhawks in the woodland areas; Buzzards circling overhead; Peregrine Falcons on Britannia Bridge.

Where to eat:
There are three cafes in Menai Bridge. The first you will reach from Uxbridge Square is Café Aethwy, which serves hot and cold drinks and snacks, home made cakes and soup. Further on is Stafford House Fine Foods, a delicatessen which also offers drinks and snacks, and slightly further on again is the Castle

Menai Suspension Bridge

Bakery and Tea Room, which offers hot and cold drinks and cakes.

Other information:
- Free parking
- No toilets at car park, public toilets in town beside bowling green

What other sights are nearby:
- Historic town and castle in Beaumaris
- Penmon Priory and Penmon
- University town of Bangor
- Anglesey Coastal Path

Appendix

A guide to Welsh pronunciation

One of the pleasures of exploring the Welsh countryside is coming across the Welsh place names and signs. Here is a simple guide to pronunciation so that asking for directions should you need to, will pose you no problems, as well as an explanation of some of the place names you may encounter on your walks.

At first sight, Welsh words may look rather difficult to pronounce but in fact, the pronunciation rules are more straightforward than for the English language.The Welsh alphabet is a little different to the English alphabet. W and Y are vowels, the letters K, Q, V, X or Z are not included, and there are a few additions, ie Ch, Dd, Ff, Ng, Ll, Ph, Rh and Th. So the alphabet looks like this:

A	H	Rh
B	I	S
C	J	T
Ch	L	Th
D	Ll	U
Dd	M	W
E	N	Y
F	O	
Ff	P	
G	Ph	
Ng	R	

Welsh vowels can be either short or long:

A   either as in 'bat' or as in 'bard'
E   either as in 'pen' or as in 'pear'
I   either as in 'mink' or as in 'mean'

O   either as in 'cog' or as in 'core'
U   either as in 'bin' or as in 'been'
W   either as in 'brook' or as in 'broom'
Y   either as in 'bin' or as in 'been'

Unfortunately, there are no simple rules to tell you when a vowel sound is short or long, but if in doubt, use the short vowel sound, unless you see a circumflex ˆ over the vowel e.g. môr.

Consonants, however, are always pronounced the same way. Unlike the English language there are no exceptions or variations to pronunciation:

B   as in 'ball'
C   as in 'cat'
Ch as in the Scottish word 'loch'
D   as in 'dig'
Dd as in 'the' or 'smooth'
F   as in 'have' like an English 'V'
Ff as in 'face' like an English 'F'
G   as in 'gold'
Ng as in 'long'
H   as in 'hat'
L   as in 'look'
Ll as an 'L' but you blow out air through your back teeth at the same time!
M as in 'man'
N   as in 'not'
P   as in 'pit'
Ph as in 'face' like an English 'F'
R   as in 'ring'
Rh like an 'R' followed by a 'huh' sound
S   as in 'sea'
T   as in 'tea'
Th as in 'think'

Mutations

To be able to read signs and place names, you do not need to understand the grammar of the Welsh language. However, it might help you to be aware that in Welsh, words that begin with certain consonants sometimes change their first letters to help with pronunciation, depending on the word that precedes it. This is known as a mutation. For example, 'bach' may become 'fach' and 'caer' may become 'gaer'. Don't worry about learning the rules, but being aware of these mutations may help you to spot words which have changed.

Place-name glossary

A lot of places in Wales have names that are not their original ones, but Anglicisations. Here are some that occur in this book, with their Welsh names alongside:

Bae Caergybi	Holyhead Bay
Caergybi	Holyhead
Cors Ddyga	Malltraeth Marsh
Eryri	Snowdonia
Niwbwrch	Newborough
Porthaethwy	Menai Bridge
Trwyn Eilian	Point Lynas
Ynys Gybi	Holy Island
Ynys Lawd	South Stack
Ynys Môn	Anglesey
Y Fali	Valley
Yr Wyddfa	Snowdon

In the Welsh language, most place-names have meanings explaining the history or location of the places themselves. The glossary below is to help you identify what's behind the names:

Aber – river mouth
Abaty – abbey
Afon – river
Bach/Fach – little
Bedd – grave
Bwlch – pass
Bryn – hill
Cae – field, enclosure
Caer/Gaer – fort, camp
Canol – centre
Capel – chapel
Carn, Carnedd – heap of stones
Carreg – crag or stone
Castell – castle or fortress
Cefn – ridge
Clogwyn – cliff
Coch/Goch – red
Coed – wood
Copa – summit
Cors/Gors – bog or marsh
Craig/graig – rock
Croes/groes – cross
Cwm – coombe
Dinas – city, fortress
Ddu – black
Dôl/Ddôl – meadow
Dŵr – water
Dyffryn – valley
Eglwys – church
Eryri – highland
Esgair – ridge
Ffordd – road
Ffynnon – well
Foel – bare hill

Galt – slope
Garth – enclosure
Glan – riverbank
Glas – blue
Glyn – deep valley
Gwyn – white
Hafod – summer dwelling
Hen – old
Hendre – winter dwelling
Isaf – lower
Llan – parish
Llyn – lake
Llys – hall or court
Lon – lane
Maen – stone
Maes/Faes – field or meadow
Mawr/Fawr – large
Melin/Felin – mill
Moel – bare hill
Môr – sea
Morfa – flat seashore
Mynydd/Fynydd – mountain
Nant – stream
Newydd – new
Ogof – cave
Pant – hollow
Parc – park
Pen – head or point
Penrhyn – promontory
Pentre – village
Plas – mansion, house
Pont/Bont – bridge
Porth/Borth – port
Pwll – pool
Rhaeadr – waterfall

Rhiw – hill
Rhos – moorland
Rhyd – ford
Sarn – causeway
Tan – under
Traeth – beach, sandy shore
Tref/Dref – town
Trwyn – peninsula
Twll – cave
Tŵr – tower
Twyni – sand dunes
Tŷ – house
Tŷ bach – toilet
Tyddyn – farmstead
Uchaf – upper
Waun – moorland
Wen – white
Wern/Gwern – alder swamp
Y, Yr – the
Yn – in
Ynys – island

Caffi/Café Vocabulary

As you try out the various cafés and tea rooms across the area, you may well encounter menus in Welsh. Most places will offer a bilingual menu, but in case you want to try ordering in Welsh, here is a short selection:

Cig moch – Bacon
Bara brith – Fruit loaf
Biscedi – Biscuit
Brechdan – Sandwich/roll
Brecwast – Breakfast
Cacen – Cake
Caws – Cheese

Coffi/goffi – Coffee
Dŵr – Water
Ffa pôb – Baked beans
Hufen iâ -Ice cream
Llefrith – Milk
Menyn – Butter
Panad o de – Cup of tea
Panad o goffi – Cup of coffee
Pot o de – Pot of tea
Pysgodyn a sglodion – Fish and Chips
Sgon – Scone
Selsig – Sausage
Siocled poeth – Hot Chocolate
Sudd oren – Orange Juice
Swgr – Sugar
Te/de – Tea
Tost – Toast
Wy – Egg

Welsh Bird Names
On your walks you may also come across interpretation boards
to help with bird identification. Here are a few common bird
names in Welsh:

Aderyn y to – House Sparrow
Alarch Dof – Mute Swan
Bran Dyddyn – Carrion Crow
Bronfraith – Song Thrush
Bwncath – Common Buzzard
Cigfran – Raven
Cnocell Fraith Fwyaf – Great Spotted Woodpecker
Cnocell Werdd – Green Woodpecker
Cog – Cuckoo
Cornchwiglen – Lapwing
Crëyr Bach – Little Egret

Crëyr Glas – Grey Heron
Cudyll Coch – Kestrel
Cwtiar – Coot
Drudwen – Starling
Dryw – Wren
Dryw Eurben – Goldcrest
Ehedydd – Skylark
Ffesant – Pheasant
Glas y Dorlan – Kingfisher
Gwalch Glas – Sparrowhawk
Gwalch y Pysgod – Osprey
Gwennol – Barn Swallow
Gwennol Ddu – Swift
Gwennol y Bondo – House Martin
Gwydd Canada – Canada Goose
Gwydd Wyllt – Greylag Goose
Gwylan Benddu – Black-headed Gull
Gwylan y Penwaig – Herring Gull
Gylfinir – Curlew
Hebog Tramor – Peregrine Falcon
Hwyaden Wyllt – Mallard
Iar Ddŵr – Moorhen
Jac y Do – Jackdaw
Ji-binc – Chaffinch
Llinos – Linnet
Llinos Werdd – Greenfinch
Llwyd y Gwrych – Dunnock
Mulfran – Cormorant
Mwyalchen – Blackbird
Nico – Goldfinch
Pâl – Puffin
Pibydd Coesgoch – Redshank
Pibydd Coeswerdd – Greenshank
Pioden – Magpie
Pioden y Môr – Oystercatcher

Robin Goch – Robin
Siff Saff – Chiffchaff
Siglen Fraith – Pied Wagtail
Siglen Lwyd – Grey Wagtail
Telor y Cyrs – Reed Warbler
Telor y Helyg – Willow Warbler
Telor yr Hesg – Sedge Warbler
Titw Cynffon-hir – Long-tailed Tit
Titw Mawr – Great Tit
Titw Penddu – Coal Tit
Titw Tomos Las – Blue Tit
Turtur Dorchog – Collared Dove
Ydfran – Rook
Ysgrech y Coed – Jay
Ysguthan – Wood Pigeon

Useful Contacts

Countryside Council for Wales
Maes-y-Ffynnon, Penrhosgarnedd, Bangor, Gwynedd LL57 2DW
Tel 01248 306 229

Forest Enterprise
Forestry Commission Wales
Victoria House, Victoria Terrace, Aberystwyth,
Ceredigion SY23 2DQ
Tel 0845 604 0945

National Trust Office for Wales
Trinity Square, Llandudno, Conwy, LL30 2DE
Tel 01492 860 123

North Wales Wildlife Trusts
376 High Street, Bangor, Gwynedd LL57 1YE
Tel 01248 351 541

RSPB North Wales Office
Maes-y-Ffynnon, Penrhosgarnedd, Bangor, Gwynedd LL57 2DW
Tel 01248 363 800

Acknowledgements

My deepest thanks go to my partner, Alan Davies, without whose incredible knowledge of the birds of northern Wales this book wouldn't have been possible. What Alan doesn't know about finding good birds in this area simply isn't worth knowing.

I also want to thank my sister Susan Kenwell, who was brave enough to accompany me on so many adventures into unknown territory to test out potential walking routes – I couldn't have asked for a better walking companion!

Many thanks to Steve Young for his outstanding bird photographs, and for the support of Julie Rogers, Keith Webster, Marc Berw-Hughes and Matthew Latham in putting together this book.

I'd also like to record my appreciation to the following for their information boards, which helped me gather material for this book:

Anglesey County Council; Countryside Council for Wales; Environment Agency Wales; RSPB; North Wales Wildlife Trust; National Trust; CADW.

Photo credits

Bird photographs: Steve Young
Other photographs: Author's own